Jus Cogens

ELEMENTS OF INTERNATIONAL LAW

Series Editors

Mark Janis is William F. Starr Professor of Law at the University of Connecticut.

Douglas Guilfoyle is Associate Professor of International and Security Law at UNSW Canberra.

Stephan Schill is Professor of International and Economic Law and Governance at the University of Amsterdam.

Bruno Simma is Professor of Law at the University of Michigan and a Judge at the Iran-US Claims Tribunal in The Hague.

Kimberley Trapp is Professor of Public International Law at University College London.

Elements of International Law represents a fresh approach in the literature of international law. It is a long series of short books. Elements adopts an objective, non-argumentative approach to its subject matter, focusing on narrowly defined core topics in international law. Eventually, the series will offer a comprehensive treatment of the whole of the field. At the same time, each individual title will be a reliable go-to source for practicing international lawyers, judges and arbitrators, government and military officers, scholars, teachers, and students engaged in the discipline of international law.

Previously Published in this Series

The European Court of Human Rights
Angelika Nussberger

International Law in the Russian Legal System
William E. Butler

The International Tribunal for the Law of the Sea
Kriangsak Kittichaisaree

Jus Cogens

Dinah Shelton

OXFORD
UNIVERSITY PRESS

Great Clarendon Street, Oxford, OX2 6DP,
United Kingdom

Oxford University Press is a department of the University of Oxford.
It furthers the University's objective of excellence in research, scholarship,
and education by publishing worldwide. Oxford is a registered trade mark of
Oxford University Press in the UK and in certain other countries

First Edition published in 2021

Impression: 1

Published in the United States of America by Oxford University Press
198 Madison Avenue, New York, NY 10016, United States of America

British Library Cataloguing in Publication Data

Data available

Library of Congress Control Number: 2020945210

ISBN 978–0–19–886595–7 (hbk.)
ISBN 978–0–19–886596–4 (pbk.)

DOI: 10.1093/law/9780198865957.001.0001

Printed and bound by
CPI Group (UK) Ltd, Croydon, CR0 4YY

Series Editors' Preface

I am delighted to welcome this wonderful contribution to our new series, Elements of International Law: Jus Cogens by Professor Dinah Shelton. When the *Elements' Editors* set out to find the best-qualified author to write our *jus cogens* volume, it was really not a difficult task of discovery. One scholar stood out: Dinah Shelton. Through a remarkable and distinguished career, Professor Shelton has secured her place as one of the most respected authorities in International Law, and her work on the important and complex role of fundamental norms in our discipline is unique and without modern parallel. All of the editors of *Elements* are honored to have Professor Shelton joining our series.

Let me briefly put Professor Shelton's book into the larger context of *Elements of International Law*. Some years ago I brought the concept of the series to John Louth and Merel Alsteen, international law editors at Oxford University Press. Together, along with co-editors Douglas Guilfoyle, Stephan Schill, Bruno Simma, and Kimberley Trapp, we structured *Elements,* chose topics, sought out the best person for each book, and edited their contributions. There are several dozen authors already working on Elements books and we anticipate about six published works in 2020, and ten or so more in each of the next years, in time numbering more than one hundred volumes.

Elements represents a fresh approach to the literature of international law. It is a long series of short books. Following the traditional path of an international law treatise, *Elements*, rather than treating the whole of the field in one increasingly heavy volume, focuses on more narrowly-defined subject matters, such as *Jus Cogens and International Law.*

There is nothing like *Elements*. It treats particular topics of international law much more extensively and in significantly more depth than traditional international law texts or encyclopedias. Each book in the *Elements* series has a relatively narrow focus and renders a comprehensive treatment of a specialized subject matter, in comparison to the more limited treatment of the same subject matter in other general works.

Like a classic textbook, *Elements* aims to provide objective statements of the law. The series does not concern itself with the academic niches filled ably by doctoral theses, nor include works which take an argumentative point of view, already well done by the OUP *Monograph* series. Except in length and integration, *Elements* is for substantive topics comparable to OUP's *Commentary* series on individual treaties: a highly reliable, objective, in-depth, and readable account of its subject.

Each book in *Elements* is exhaustively footnoted in respect of international legal practice and scholarship, e.g., treaties, diplomatic practice, decisions by international and municipal courts and arbitral tribunals, resolutions and acts of international organizations, and commentary by the most authoritative jurists. *Elements* adopts an objective, non-argumentative approach to its many subject matters and constitutes a reliable go-to source for practicing international lawyers, judges and arbitrators, government and military lawyers, and scholars, teachers, and students engaged in the discipline of international law.

All of us committed to *Elements* – authors, editors, publishers – hope that our series will make a real difference to international law and to the rule of law. We are so delighted to have Professor Shelton's *Jus Cogens* as one of our earliest books in the series. Not only because of its accomplished author, but because *jus cogens* is both one of the more difficult-to-understand concepts in our discipline and one of the most important, laying a foundation for the other norms of International Law. I am sure you will find Professor Shelton's book to be an important guide to understanding this concept in depth.

Mark Janis
Editor-in-Chief, Editorial Board,
Elements of International Law
William F Starr Professor of Law,
University of Connecticut
31 August 2020
Hartford, Connecticut

Preface

This book has been a long time in preparation, especially considering the many years of teaching international law and thinking about its sources. I have previously written about the topic of *jus cogens*, including in the *Netherlands Yearbook of International Law*, 2015, and the *American Journal of International Law*, among others. Inevitably, some of the basics of this volume draw upon those earlier publications. I have listed these in full below and am grateful for and wish to acknowledge them here.

I am also very appreciative of Mark Janis's invitation to embark on the work of writing this work as part of the series *Elements of International Law*. Undertaking the study has required me to update my previous writings and to follow closely the recent work of the UN International Law Commission on the topic. I hope I have done justice to the excellent reports of its special rapporteur, Mr Dire Tladi, on peremptory norms of general international law (*jus cogens*). There are many new elements in his four reports and the responses to them from states and other members of the ILC. I hope they are all adequately treated herein. Any errors are entirely my responsibility, of course.

As is always the case with my research and writing, I owe an enormous debt of gratitude to the law librarians at the George Washington University Law School. They are always unfailing in their expertise and assistance. Thanks also to OUP and Newgen for its work on editing and publishing this work.

1. Chapters 1, 2, 3, 5, 6, and 7 draw upon materials published in Dinah Shelton, 'Sherlock Holmes and the mystery of jus cogens', 46 *Netherlands Yearbook of International Law*, (2015) 23–50. Reprinted with permission.
2. Chapters 1,2,3,5, and 6 draw upon materials published in Dinah Shelton, 'International Law and "Relative Normativity"' in M.D Evans (ed.), *International Law*, (4th edn, OUP 2014) 137–166.
3. Chapter 2 draws upon material published in Dinah Shelton, 'Normative Hierarchy and International Law', (2006) 100 *American Journal of International Law*, 291–326. Reprinted with permission.

4. The book reviews: R. Kolb, *Peremptory International Law (Jus Cogens): A General Inventory* (Oxford and Portland, OR, Hart 2015) xv, 148, Bibliography, Index; and T. Weatherall, *Jus Cogens: International Law and Social Contract* (Cambridge University Press 2015), xliv, 509, Index.

5. Dinah Shelton, 'Resolving conflicts between human rights and environmental protection: Is there a hierarchy?' in E. de Wet and J. Vidmar (eds), *Hierarchy in International Law: The Place of Human Rights* (OUP, 2012), 206–235.

6. 'The Legal Status of Normative Pronouncements of Human Rights Treaty Bodies' in H. Hestermeyer et al (eds) *Coexistence, Cooperation and Solidarity: liber Amicorum Rudiger Wolfrum*, vol I (Brill Publishers, 2011), 553–577.

7. 'Hiérarchie des normes en droit international des droits de l'homme,' 26 *La protection des espaces- L'Observateur des Nations Unies*, 237 (2009-1).

8. 'Mettre en balance les droits : vers une hiérarchie des norms en droit international des droits de l'homme,' in E. Bribosia & L. Hennebel (eds) *Classer les droits de l'homme* (BRUYLANT 2004) 153.

Table of Contents

List of Abbreviations

ASR	Articles on State Responsibility
ATCA	US Alien Tort Claim Act
CJEC	Court of Justice of the European Union
DRC	Democratic Republic of the Congo
ECHR	European Convention on Human Rights
ECtHR	European Court of Human Rights
EU	European Union
IACtHR	Inter-American Court of Human Rights
ICC	International Criminal Court
ICCPR	International Covenant on Civil and Political Rights
ICJ	International Court of Justice
ICTR	International Criminal Tribunal for Rwanda
ICTY	International Criminal Tribunal for the Former Yugoslavia
ILC	International Law Commission
OAS	Organization of American States
PCIJ	Permanent Court of International Justice
SR	Special Rapporteur
UN	United Nations
UNCLOS	United Nations Convention on the Law of the Sea
US	United States
VCLT	Vienna Convention on the Law of Treaties 1969

1
Introduction*

Publicists have long sought to develop a theory that would serve to constrain the claimed unlimited State discretion, in the exercise of sovereignty, to accept or reject an international treaty norm or developing customary international law. The doctrine of peremptory norms (*jus cogens*) is the primary theory developed in this effort. Notably, however, the norms most often cited as *jus cogens* have been universally accepted as customary international law or are contained in treaties adhered to by all or nearly all States. Breach of any such norm is a violation of international law; calling the norm *jus cogens* seems to add little—unless the consequences of violating such norms are enhanced or differ in other ways from breaches of 'normal' international law.

On the positive side, however, it may be speculated that at least some support for the development of international criminal law has been based in the desire to limit the ability to opt out of particularly important international norms. In practice, it seems that each lawyer, scholar, and judge brings a particular vision to the issue of identifying what are the important or essential international norms that States should be unable to opt out of or reject. In fact, the content of *jus cogens* involve considerable subjectivity. Nonetheless, this does not diminish the value of *jus cogens* as a representation of the idea that there is an international society with core values. In the end, belief that *jus cogens* exists may be its most important attribute, ensuring that it has some, albeit ill-defined impact.

Available evidence suggests that international *jus cogens* originated as a construct of writers, in this case in the efforts of early publicists to explain an emerging legal system governing sovereign states, where rulers often claimed absolute power unrestrained by law.[1] Scholars sought to

---

* This chapter draws upon materials published in: Dinah Shelton, 'Sherlock Holmes and the mystery of jus cogens', 46 Netherlands Yearbook of International Law, (2015) 23–50. Reprinted with permission. Dinah Shelton, 'International Law and "Relative Normativity"' in M.D Evans (ed.), International Law, (4th edn, OUP 2014) 137–166.

[1] For historical development of *jus cogens*, see, A.G. Robledo, 1982a, *El ius cogens internacional* (Mexico, Universidad Nacional Autónoma de México); and A.G. Robledo, 1982b, 'Le ius cogens international: Sa genese, sa nature, ses fonctions', *172 Recueil des Cours*, 10–68.

understand the nature and source of obligations that could limit the power of governments internally and internationally, binding them to a set of legal norms to which they did not necessarily express consent.[2] Finding the source of such international obligations became a perpetual quest.

Early writers also foresaw problems of hierarchy that would surface with the emergence of conflicting obligations. In attempting to propound a coherent legal system, they turned to analogies from private law, general principles, legal theory, moral and legal philosophy, and religion. They developed the notion of a 'higher' law, from which the doctrine *jus cogens* emerged. Since then, proponents have argued strongly for the existence and functions of *jus cogens* in international law, while critics have expressed scepticism about the reality or practical value of the concept.[3]

The only references to peremptory norms in positive law are found in the Vienna conventions on the law of treaties,[4] further discussed in section 2.3. Article 53 of the 1969 Vienna Convention on the Law of Treaties (VCLT), concerning treaties between States, provides that a treaty will be void 'if, at the time of its conclusion, it conflicts with a peremptory norm of general international law'. The 1986 Convention on Treaties between States and International Organizations or between International Organizations is similar in content. Anticipating the VCLT provisions are the writings of classic and modern publicists proposing various sources and functions of *jus cogens*, as discussed in the chapters that follow. They reveal the cultural importance of *jus cogens*, but also the very limited role it plays in dispute settlement or enforcement of norms.

[2] For a discussion of early attempts to ascertain limits on the exercise of sovereignty, see S. Kadelbach, 2006, at 21; Haimbaugh, 1987, at 207–211.

[3] For critical assessments, see, e.g. Schwarzenberger 1967, at 29–30; Schwelb 1967, at 961 (referring to 'the vagueness, the elasticity, and the dangers of the concept of international *jus cogens*'); J. Sztucki, 1974, *Jus cogens and the Vienna Convention on the Law of Treaties* (Vienna, Springer); G.A. Christenson, 1988, '*Jus cogens*: Guarding interests fundamental to international society', *28 Virginia J. Int'l Law*, 585–648; G. Danilenko, 1991, 'International *jus cogens*: Issues of law-making', *2 Eur. J. Int'l Law*, 42–65; M. Weisburd, 1995, 'The emptiness of the concept of *jus cogens*, as illustrated by the war in Bosnia-Herzegovina', *17 Michigan J. Int'l Law*, 1–51.

[4] Vienna Convention on the Law of Treaties, 1155 UNTS 331; 1986 Vienna Convention on the Law of Treaties between States and International Organizations or between International Organizations, UN Doc. A/CONF.129/15.

2
The Origins and Sources of *Jus Cogens**

Jus cogens has been developed largely by international legal scholarship,[1] which has attempted to identify the theoretical foundations of a world juridical order. Every classic author in the field of international law expounds a theory of the source of obligation and the nature of international law. They typically distinguish between voluntary or consensual law and compulsory norms that bind a state independently of its will. Some early writers found the source of compulsory law in divine or religious law, binding all humans and human institutions.[2] A related theory derives the concept of *jus cogens* from general principles of law, noting the existence of overriding public policy and superior norms in all legal systems. Finally, positivists rely on state consent for the origin, content, and functions of *jus cogens*. Each of these conceptual approaches is discussed in the following subsections.

2.1 Natural Law

For most classical writers, there existed three levels of legal obligation: *jus dispositivum* or voluntary law, divine law, and *jus naturale necessarium* (necessary natural law), the last mentioned being the highest category. Gentili[3]

---

* This chapter draws upon materials published in: Dinah Shelton, 'Sherlock Holmes and the mystery of jus cogens', 46 Netherlands Yearbook of International Law, (2015) 23–50. Reprinted with permission. Dinah Shelton, 'International Law and "Relative Normativity"' in M.D Evans (ed.), International Law, (4th edn, OUP 2014) 137–166.

[1] For a history of this doctrinal development, see A.G. Robledo, 1982, *El ius cogens internacional* (Mexico, Universidad Nacional Autónoma de México); and A.G. Robledo, 1982, 'Le ius cogens international: Sa genese, sa nature, ses fonctions', *172 Recueil des Cours*, 10–68.

[2] The earliest evidence of treaty practice indicates that the entirety of international obligation was perceived to originate in divine mandates, and any trespass of borders or subjugation of one country by another was regarded as a violation of the divine established order and a grave offence which could lead to immediate sanction by the gods of the breaching party. See A. Amnon, 2012, *Tracing the Earliest Recorded Concepts of International Law: The Ancient Near East (2500–330 BC)* (Leiden, Martinus Nijhoff).

[3] A. Gentili, 1933, *De iure belli libri tres* (Oxford, Clarendon Press; London, H. Milford).

connected natural law to the law of nations, influencing Grotius who gave primary place to natural law, even over divine law: 'The law of nature, again, is unchangeable—even in the sense that it cannot be changed by God. Measureless as is the power of God, nevertheless it can be said that there are certain things over which that power does not extend.'[4] If such principles of natural law were unchangeable even by God, they necessarily bound all sovereigns on earth: 'Since this law is not subject to change and the obligations which it imposes are necessary and indispensable, Nations cannot alter it by agreement, nor individually or mutually release themselves from it.'[5] So, while voluntary or consent-based law could be created by the express or tacit will of states, such law could not override natural law.

Wolff[6] and Vattel[7] agreed that there existed 'necessary law' by which they meant it was binding and overriding of state consent. This law was natural to all states and made illegal all treaties and customs which contravened this necessary law. Wolff's necessary law of nations[8] included the immutable laws of justice, the 'sacred law', which nations and sovereigns are bound to respect and follow in all their actions.[9] Pufendorf[10] and Vattel also relied on natural law 'no less binding on states, on men united in political society, than on individuals'.[11] They saw the natural law of nations as a particular science, 'consisting in a just and rational application of the law of nature to the affairs and conduct of nations or sovereigns'.[12] The distinction between *jus dispositivum* and the 'necessary principles of international law that bind all states regardless of consent' lies in the origin of the latter in the natural law of reason:

---

[4] H. Grotius, 1625, *On the Law of War and Peace (De jure belli ac pacis libri tres)* (1646 edn transl. by F.W. Kelsey, 1925, Oxford, Clarendon Press).

[5] Ibid.

[6] C. Wolff, 1764, *Jus gentium methodo scientifica pertractorum* [*A scientific method for understanding the law of nations*] (transl. by J.H. Drake, S.J. Brown, ed., London, Clarendon Press), para. 5.

[7] E. de Vattel, 1758, *Le droit des gens ou principes de la loi naturelle* (London, Neuchâtel), para. 9.

[8] J. Chitty, 1849, 'Preface', in E. de Vattel (ed.), *The Law of Nations; Or Principles of the Law of Nature Applied to the Conduct and Affairs of Nations and Sovereigns* (transl. and intro. by J. Chitty, 7th Am. edn, Philadelphia, T. & J.W. Johnson Law Booksellers), at ix (citing C. Wolff, 1764), '[T]he law of nations certainly belongs to the law of nature: it is, therefore, on account of its origin, called the Natural, and, by reason of its obligatory force, the necessary law of nations.'

[9] Ibid., at xiii.

[10] S. Pufendorf, 1710, *Of law of Nature and Nations* (Oxford, L. Lichfield, for A. & J. Churchill), at Book ii, ch. iii, Sect. 23.

[11] Chitty (n 8), at xi.

[12] Ibid.

> We use the term necessary Law of Nations for that law which results from applying the natural law to Nations. It is necessary, because Nations are absolutely bound to observe it ... This same law is called by Grotius and his followers the internal Law of Nations, inasmuch as it is binding upon the conscience of Nations ... It is by the application of this principle that a distinction can be made between lawful and unlawful treaties or conventions and between customs which are innocent and reasonable and those which are unjust and deserving of condemnation.[13]

Suy claims that the actual words *jus cogens* are not found in any text prior to the nineteenth century,[14] although the idea of a law binding irrespective of the will of individual parties is common through 'the whole theory and philosophy of law'.[15] Early twentieth-century publicists, such as Lassa Oppenheim and William Hall, continued to assert that states could not abrogate certain 'universally recognized principles' by mutual agreement.[16] The rise of positivism reduced although it did not entirely eliminate natural law from theoretical discourse.

2.2 Public Policy: Logical or Legal Necessity

Necessity took on another meaning for authors who focused their attention on positing the fundamental needs of any legal system and on the definition of law itself. Several writers suggested that any society operating under law must have fundamental rules allowing for no dissent if the existence of the law and society is to be maintained. According to Rozakis, the *ratio legis* of *jus cogens* is to protect the common concerns of the subjects of law, the values and interests considered indispensable by a society at a given time.[17] Organized society creates an ordering of norms, but only when there is a minimum degree of community feeling does it elevate certain values as

---

[13] de Vattel (n 8), pp. 7 and 9.

[14] He cites first the 1847 Pandecten of van Gluck I who refers to those laws which categorically prescribe an action or prohibit it and whose binding force is absolute. E. Suy, 1967, 'The concept of *jus cogens* in public international law', in *The Concept of Jus Cogens in International Law: Papers and Proceedings*, Report of Conference organized by the Carnegie Endowment for International Peace, Lagonissi, Greece (April 1966), at 19.

[15] Ibid., at 18.

[16] W. Hall, 1924, *A Treatise on International Law* (8th edn, Oxford, Clarendon), pp. 382–383; L. Oppenheim, 1905, *International Law* (London, Longmans), p. 528.

[17] C. Rozakis, 1976, *The Concept of Jus Cogens in the Law of Treaties* (Amsterdam, North Holland Publishing Co.), p. 2.

necessary, with primacy over others.[18] *Jus cogens* in international law therefore starts to appear in positive law as international society develops from relatively unorganized into an increasingly organized one with common interests and values.[19]

The existence of an international legal system means that public policy requires states to conform to those principles whose non-observance would render illusory the very concept of an international society of states or the concept of international law itself, such as the principles of sovereign equality and *pacta sunt servanda*. Public policy—*ordre public*—may be defined by its effects, that is, the impossibility for individuals of opting out, or by its objective: to protect the essential interest of the state and establish the legal foundations of the economic and moral order of the society.[20] This implies limiting the will of the individual to meet the essential needs of the community.

According to Tomuschat, such a society of fundamental principles has emerged gradually in international relations:

> [t]he fact is that the cohesive legal bonds tying States to one another have considerably strengthened since the coming into force of the United Nations Charter; ... a community model of international society would seem to come closer to reality than at any time before in history.[21]

States live within a legal framework of a few basic rules that nonetheless allow them considerable freedom of action. Such a framework has become necessary in the light of global problems threatening human survival in an unprecedented fashion. Recalcitrant states would not only profit by rejecting regulatory regimes adopted by the overwhelming majority of states, they would also threaten the effectiveness of such regimes and pose risks to all humanity.[22]

---

[18] Carnegie Endowment for International Peace, The Concept of Jus Cogens in International Law: Papers and Proceedings (n 14), at 10.

[19] Ibid., at 12.

[20] H. de Page, 1962, *Traité élémentaire de droit civil belge* (Brussels, Bruylant), p. 111.

[21] C. Tomuschat, 1993, 'Obligations arising for states without or against their will', *241 Recueil des Cours*, 191–374, at 210–211.

[22] Ibid. The emergence of global resource crises, such as the widespread depletion of commercial fish stocks, destruction of the stratospheric ozone layer, and anthropogenic climate change, has produced growing concern about the 'free rider', the holdout state that benefits from legal regulation accepted by others while enhancing its own profits through continued utilization of the resource or by ongoing production and sale of banned substances.

In this public order theory, *jus cogens* norms exist as imperative and hierarchically superior to other international law in order to promote the interests of the international community as a whole and preserve core values. According to von Verdross, this is inherent in all legal systems: 'A truly realistic analysis of the law shows us that every positive juridical order has its roots in the ethics of a certain community, that it cannot be understood apart from its moral basis.'[23] As a consequence, the principle of immoral agreements is recognized in every national legal order. In his third report on the law of treaties in 1958, rapporteur Fitzmaurice appeared to see *jus cogens* from the public order perspective, as he asserted that rules of *jus cogens* 'possess a common characteristic', namely 'that they involve not only legal rules but considerations of morals and of international good order'.[24] An international tribunal might refuse to recognize a treaty or to apply it where the treaty 'is clearly contrary to humanity, good morals, or to international good order or the recognized ethics of international behaviour'.[25] The origin of *jus cogens* would thus seem to lie in the sociology or logic of law which requires compliance with essential rules on which the system itself is based; it does not, however, indicate the process by which such rules may be identified on the international level.

2.3 General Principles of Law

The theory that finds the origin of *jus cogens* in general principles of law recognized in all legal systems, is linked to logical or legal necessity, but is more in keeping with international law doctrine on sources of law. Private agreements contrary to public policy or *ordre public* are void, voidable, or unenforceable. The rules of public policy are an essential part of the legal and social framework on which every effective legal system, including the international one, ultimately rests.[26] In its study on fragmentation of international law, the International Law Commission (ILC) Study Group addressed *jus cogens*, noting that the idea of hierarchy of norms 'has found its

---

[23] A. von Verdross, 1937, 'Forbidden treaties in international law: Comments on Professor Garner's report on "The Law of Treaties"', *31 Am. J. Int'l Law*, 571–577, at 574–576.
[24] G.G. Fitzmaurice, Special Rapporteur, Third report on the law of treaties, 10th sess. of the ILC, A/CN.4/SER.A/1958/Add.l, 1958, at 41.
[25] Ibid., at 28.
[26] Georg Schwarzenberger, 1965, 'International Jus Cogens' *43 Tex. L. Rev.* 455, at 457.

expression in one way or another in all legal systems.[27] Like many authors, the Study Group pointed to the Roman law distinction between *jus cogens* or *jus strictum* and *jus dispositivum* and the maxim *jus publicum privatorum pactis mutari non potest*.[28]

Domestic laws generally provide for the invalidity of agreements that conflict with public policy or *ordre public*. German authors writing in the early 1930s referred to *jus cogens* as general principles of law which are recognized as overriding norms by all civilized nations.[29] For some French scholars, humanitarian rules also belong to general principles of law from which no derogation is possible.[30] In Lauterpacht's view, the illegality of the object of the treaty and consequently the nullity of the agreement would result from 'inconsistency with such overriding principles of international law which may be regarded as constituting principles of international public policy (*ordre international public*)'.[31] These principles need not necessarily be codified or crystallized. Lauterpacht asserts that 'overriding principles of international law', such as the suppression of slavery, 'may be regarded as constituting principles of international public policy (*ordre international public*). These principles . . . may be expressive of rules of international morality so cogent that an international tribunal would consider them forming a part of those principles of law generally recognized by civilized nations which the ICJ is bound to apply [under] its Statute'.[32]

In McNair's classic work on the law of treaties, the author found it 'difficult to imagine any society, whether of individuals or of States whose law sets no limit whatever to freedom of contract'.[33] Every civilized community

---

[27] International Law Commission, Fragmentation of international law: difficulties arising from the diversification and expansion of international law, Report of the Study Group of the International Law Commission, 58th Sess., UN Doc. A/CN.4/L.682, 13 April 2006, at 181.

[28] Ibid., 182. *Jus publicum* was not only public law, but all rules are important to the society.

[29] F.A. von der Heydte, 1932, 'Die Erscheinungsformen des Zwischenstaatlichen Rechts: *jus cogens* und jus dispositivum im Volkerrecht', *16 Zeitschrift für Völkerrecht*, 461–487. The author cited, in particular, the rules indispensable and necessary to the existence of every legal order, e.g. *pacta sunt servanda* and the obligation to make reparation for damages.

[30] L. Delbez, 1964, *Les principes generaux du droit international public* (3rd edn, Paris, Pichon et Durand-Auzias), pp. 317–318. 'The object of a treaty is unlawful when the obligations it contains are contrary to prior conventional obligations, rules of customary law or rules based on universal morality of an imperative character.' See also L. Cavare, 1962, *Droit international public positif* (2nd edn, Paris, Pedone), p. 69 (agreements cannot be contrary to 'le droit commun de l'humanité'); and P. Reuter, 1961, 'Principes de droit international public', *103 Recueil des Cours, Hague Academy Int'l Law*, 425–655, at 466–467.

[31] H. Lauterpacht, Special Rapporteur, Report on the law of treaties, UN Doc. A/CN.4/63, 24 March 1953.

[32] Ibid., para. 4.

[33] A.D. McNair, 1961, *Law of Treaties* (Oxford, Clarendon Press), pp. 213–214.

contains norms from which no derogation is allowed and the community of states is no exception. This suggests that he viewed *jus cogens* as originating in general principles of law, but he goes on to indicate that the specific content of such rules emerges from the consent of states. Where there is a conflict between a treaty and a norm of customary international law, McNair concludes that certain of these norms 'cannot be set aside or modified by contracting States ... they consist of rules which have been accepted, either expressly by treaty or tacitly by custom, as being necessary to protect the public interests of the society of States or to maintain the standards of public morality recognized by them'.[34]

2.4 Consent

In the nineteenth century, a notion of international law emerged that was based strictly on the consent of states.[35] Nevertheless authors from the beginning of the twentieth century continued to assert the existence of fundamental norms (*Grundnorms*)[36] sometimes founded on *la solidarité naturelle*,[37] but more often contending that states themselves had recognized peremptory norms and their effect in customary international law. Oppenheim stated in 1905 that in his view 'a number of "universally recognised principles" of international law existed which rendered any conflicting treaty void and that the peremptory effect of such principles was itself a unanimously recognized customary rule of international law'.[38] Similarly, Hall stated that:

> [t]he requirement that contracts shall be in conformity with law invalidates, or at least renders voidable, all agreements which are at variance with the fundamental principles of international law and their

---

[34] Ibid., p. 215.

[35] 'Les règles de droit international n'ont pas un caractère imperatif. Le droit international admet en conséquence qu'un traité peut avoir n'importe quel contenu', P. Guggenheim, 1953, *Traité de droit international public* (Genf, Georg), pp. 57–58. See also G. Morelli, 1951, *Nozioni di diritto internazionale* (Padova, CEDAM), p. 37; *The Case of the S.S. Lotus*, PCIJ, Judgment 9 of 7 September 1927, at 18.

[36] H. Kelsen, 1945, *General Theory of Law and State* (Cambridge, Harvard University Press), pp. 110 ff.

[37] G. Scelle, 1932, *Précis de droit des gens* (Paris, Recueil Sirey), Première Partie, p. 3; and G. Scelle, 1948, *Cours de droit international public* (Paris Dormat-Montchrestien), pp. 5 ff.

[38] Oppenheim (n 16), p. 528.

undisputed applications, and with the arbitrary usages which have acquired decisive authority.[39]

In 1934, Judge Schücking asserted that the League of Nations would not have embarked on the codification of international law 'if it were not possible to create *jus cogens*, the effect of which would be that, once States have agreed on certain rules of law, and have also given an undertaking that these rules may not be altered by some only of their number, any act adopted in contravention of that undertaking would be automatically void'.[40]

A strictly voluntarist view of international law rejects the notion that a state may be bound to an international legal rule without its consent and thus does not recognize a collective interest that is capable of overriding the will of an individual member of the society. States are deemed to construct the corpus of international law either through agreements or through repeated practice out of a sense of legal obligation.[41] The Permanent Court of International Justice (PCIJ), in one of its first decisions, stated that '[t]he rules of law binding upon States ... emanate from their own free will as expressed in conventions or by usages generally accepted as expressing principles of law'.[42] As recently as 1986, the ICJ reaffirmed this approach in respect to the acquisition of weaponry by states. In the *Nicaragua* judgment the Court stated:

> In international law there are no rules, other than such rules as may be accepted by the State concerned, by treaty or otherwise, whereby the level of armaments of a sovereign State can be limited, and this principle is valid for all States without exception.[43]

Some legal theorists have long objected that the source of international obligation cannot lie in consent, but must be based on a prior, fundamental norm that imposes a duty to comply with obligations freely accepted

---

[39] Hall (n 16), p. 382.

[40] See, *Oscar Chinn* case, 1934 PCIJ (ser. A/B) No. 63, at 149–150 (Schücking, J. dissenting).

[41] See L. Henkin, 1989, 'International law: Politics, values and functions', *216 Recueil des Cours*, 9–416, at 45; P. Weil, 1983, 'Towards relative normativity in international law?', *77 Am. J. Int'l L.*, 413–442; G. Danilenko, 1991, 'International *jus cogens*: Issues of law-making', *2 Eur. J. Int'l Law* 42–65, at 42; I.I. Lukashuk, 1989, 'The principle pacta sunt servanda and the nature of obligation under international law', *83 Am. J. Int'l Law*, 513–518.

[42] *Lotus*, Judgment No. 9, 1927, PCIJ, Ser A, No. 10, at 18.

[43] Military and Paramilitary Activities in and against Nicaragua (*Nicaragua v United States of America*), Merits, Judgment, ICJ Reports 1986, at 14, para. 269.

(Kelsen, 1945). Without a source of this norm outside consent there is an unavoidable circularity of reasoning. A natural law origin of international obligation was dominant among scholars until the nineteenth century, when positivism and an emphasis on the sovereignty of states emerged in theory and practice.[44]

Most contemporary commentators continue to view *jus cogens* through the prism of state consent.[45] Specifically, states may identify peremptory norms in treaties, accept them as a higher form of customary international law, or derive from them general principles of municipal law.[46] In practice, few if any examples can be found where states have expressly indicated their intent to identify or create a peremptory norm; identification is thus by implication. Yet, the positivist approach to identifying *jus cogens*, if not to explaining its origin, appears accepted by the International Court of Justice (ICJ). In *Arrest Warrant Case* the Court concluded that the prohibition against torture is a norm of *jus cogens* based on 'widespread international practice and on the *opinio juris* of States'.[47]

It is unclear how, in a consent-based system, peremptory norms bind those who object to the very concept of *jus cogens* or to a notion that such norms can be identified by a large majority and imposed on dissenters. The International Law Commission Commentary to Article 53 VCLT suggests that peremptory norms need not achieve universal acceptance to create a binding international consensus; it is sufficient if a 'very large majority' of representative states accept the norms as non-derogable.[48] The positivist concept of peremptory norms thus reaches a conundrum in having a consensual process with a non-consensual result—the imposition of rules adopted by a large majority of dissenting states. Even if states consented to a consensus-based source of international lawmaking, this would not preclude them from withdrawing their consent at will.[49] In fact, it is difficult to

---

[44] See ch. 1.

[45] M.N. Shaw, 2008, *International Law* (5th edn, Cambridge, Cambridge University Press), p. 97: '[O]nly rules based on custom or treaties may form the foundation of *jus cogens* norms.'

[46] See, e.g. M. Byers, 1997, 'Conceptualizing the relationship between *jus cogens* and erga omnes rules', 66 *Nordic J. Int'l Law*, 211–239, at 212 (*jus cogens* rules are derived from the process of customary international law).

[47] *Questions Relating to the Obligation to Prosecute or Extradite (Belgium v Senegal)*, ICJ, Judgment of 20 July 2012, at para. 99.

[48] See Restatement (Third) of Foreign Relations of the United States, para. 102, n. 6. The Restatement cites the UN Conference on the Law of Treaties, Report of the proceedings of the Committee of the Whole, UN Doc. A/CONF.39/11, 21 May 1968, at 471–472 (comments of the chairman).

[49] See J. Sztucki, 1974, *Jus cogens and the Vienna Convention on the Law of Treaties* (Vienna, Springer), p. 97.

reconcile peremptory norms that bind dissenting states with the positivist theory of international law.[50]

The extent to which the system has moved and may still move towards the imposition of global public policy on non-consenting states remains highly debated, but the need for limits on state freedom of action seems to be increasingly recognized. International legal instruments and doctrine now often refer to the 'common interest of humanity'[51] or 'common concern of mankind' to identify broad concerns that could form part of international public policy. References are also more frequent to 'the international community' as an entity or authority of collective action.[52] In addition, multilateral international agreements increasingly contain provisions that affect non-party states, either providing incentives to adhere to the norms, or allowing parties to take coercive measures that in practice require conforming behaviour of states not adhering to the treaty. The UN Charter itself contains a list of fundamental principles and in Article 2(6) asserts that these may be imposed on non-parties if necessary to ensure international peace and security.

It should be noted that the problem of dissenting states is not as widespread as might be assumed. First, the obligations deemed basic to the international community—to refrain from the use of force against another state, to peacefully settle disputes, and to respect human rights, fundamental freedoms, and self-determination—are conventional obligations contained in the UN Charter, to which all member states have consented. All states have accepted the humanitarian conventions on the laws of war which express customary international law. The multilateral regimes for the oceans, outer space, and key components of the environment (climate change, protection of the ozone layer, and biological diversity) are widely accepted. Thus in most cases the problem is one of ensuring compliance by states that have freely consented to the obligations in question and not one of imposing obligations on dissenting states.

---

[50] See ibid., p. 64. '[T]he introduction of a consensual ingredient into the concept of *jus cogens* leads inevitably, in the ultimate instance, to the very negation of that concept.' See also *Siderman de Blake v Republic of Argentina*, 965 F.2d 699, 715 (9th Cir. 1992) (stating that *jus cogens* norms 'transcend ... consent').

[51] See, UNCLOS, Art. 137(2); Treaty on Principles Governing the Activities of States in the Exploration and Use of Outer Space, Including the Moon and Other Celestial Bodies (1967), pmbl., para. 2.

[52] See, e.g. Art. 53, VCLT; Arts 136–137 UNCLOS.

3

The Law of Treaties*

3.1 Drafting the VCLT

Peremptory norms/*jus cogens* entered positive law with the Vienna treaties on treaties. *Jus cogens* was first included in the work of the ILC with the Third Report of G.G. Fitzmaurice, Special Rapporteur on the Law of Treaties, under the heading 'legality of the object'.[1] The first two *Special Rapporteurs* on the law of treaties, Brierly[2] and Lauterpacht,[3] supported the notion of peremptory norms in international law.[4] During ILC work on the law of treaties, however, most of the members joined the ILC's fourth Special Rapporteur on treaty law, Sir Humphrey Waldock, who sought to reconcile *jus cogens* with the doctrine of positivism. They spent little time speculating on the origin of *jus cogens*. The final ILC draft on the law of treaties was produced by Waldock.

The work of the International Law Commission on the law of treaties was based essentially on the notion of barring illegal agreements as a general principle of law. The ILC's first Special Rapporteur on the law of treaties, Brierly, did not refer to *jus cogens*, but did speak of contractual limitations.[5] The first report of the second ILC Special Rapporteur, H. Lauterpacht, proposed an article on *jus cogens*,[6] arguing that:

> the voidance of contractual agreements whose object is illegal is a general principle of law. As such it must find a place in a codification of the law of

---

* This chapter draws upon materials published in: Dinah Shelton, 'Sherlock Holmes and the mystery of jus cogens', 46 Netherlands Yearbook of International Law, (2015) 23–50. Reprinted with permission. Dinah Shelton, 'International Law and "Relative Normativity"' in M.D Evans (ed.), International Law, (4th edn, OUP 2014) 137–166.
    [1] A/CN.4/114; see 1958 *Yearbook of the International Law Commission Vol. II: Documents of the Tenth Session including the Report of the Commission to the General Assembly*, at 26–27.
    [2] J.L. Brierly, 1936, 'Régles générales de droit de la paix', *58 Recueil des Cours*, 5–242, at 218–219.
    [3] H. Lauterpacht, 1937, 'Régles générales de droit de la paix', *62 Recueil des Cours*, 95–422, at 153ff.
    [4] Ibid., at 306–307.
    [5] J.L. Brierly, Special Rapporteur, Report on the law of treaties, UN Doc. A/CN.4/23, 14 April 1950, at 246 ff.
    [6] H. Lauterpacht, Special Rapporteur, Report on the law of treaties, UN Doc. A/CN.4/63, 24 March 1953.

treaties. This is so although there are no instances in international judicial and arbitral practice of a treaty being declared void on account of the illegality of its object.[7]

In the ILC report submitted to the Vienna Conference on the Law of Treaties, the ILC stated that it had become increasingly difficult to sustain the proposition that there is no rule of international law from which states cannot at their own free will derogate.[8] The law of treaties thus must accept that there are certain rules from which states are not competent to withdraw, and which may be changed only by another rule of the same character.[9] The ILC also stated that although there is no simple criterion by which to identify a general rule of international law as having the character of *jus cogens*, the particular nature of the subject matter with which it deals may give it the character of *jus cogens*.[10]

Article 53 VCLT, concerning treaties between states, provides that a treaty will be void 'if, at the time of its conclusion, it conflicts with a peremptory norm of general international law'. Such a norm is defined by the VCLT as one 'accepted and recognized by the international community of states as a whole as a norm from which no derogation is permitted and which can be modified only by a subsequent norm having the same character'. Article 64 adds that the emergence of a new peremptory norm of general international law will render void any existing treaty in conflict with the norm. No clear agreement was reached during the VCLT negotiations nor has one emerged since then about the content of *jus cogens*.

The final version of Article 53 VCLT[11] was adopted by a majority of 87 votes in favour, with 8 votes against,[12] and 12 abstentions.[13] Because of this division, and the specific formulation of the article, René Jean Dupuy, in

---

[7] Ibid., para. 5.

[8] International Law Commission, Report of the International Law Commission on the work of the second part of its 17th sess., 17th sess. of the ICL, UN Doc. A/6309/Rev.1, 3–28 January 1966, at 247 ff.

[9] Ibid.

[10] Ibid.

[11] The draft article was adopted at the Vienna Conference largely as suggested, save for the addition of the words 'accepted and recognised by the international community of States as a whole'. UN Conference on the Law of Treaties, Summary records of the plenary meeting and of the meetings of the Committee of the Whole, 1st Sess., A/CONF.39/11, 1968, at 471.

[12] Australia, Belgium, France, Liechtenstein, Luxembourg, Monaco, Switzerland, and Turkey. UN Conference on the Law of Treaties, Summary records of the plenary meeting and of the meetings of the Committee of the Whole, 2nd Sess., A/CONF.39/11/Add.1, 12 May 1969, at 107.

[13] New Zealand, Norway, Portugal, Senegal, South Africa, Tunisia, United Kingdom, Gabon, Ireland, Japan, Malaysia, and Malta. Ibid.

1966 a member of the Holy See's delegation to the Vienna Conference, noted that the inclusion of Article 53 in the VCLT sanctioned the 'positivization of international law'.[14] Despite the majority being in favour of the VCLT with Article 53 on *jus cogens,* the ILC decided to appoint a new rapporteur on the topic in 2015. He noted in his first report that 'the contours and legal effects of *jus cogens* remain ill-defined and contentious'.[15] He could also have reported that there is very little case law invoking the concept to impeach the validity of a treaty.

The second treaty on the law of treaties echoed the first one. The drafting of the second treaty on treaties, the 1986 Vienna Convention on the Law of Treaties between States and International Organizations, indicated continued controversy over the concept of norms *jus cogens.* The text proposed by the ILC included provisions on *jus cogens* modelled after the 1969 VCLT. The commentary called the prohibition of the illegal use of armed force embodied in the UN Charter 'the most reliable known example of a peremptory norm' and also claimed that the notion of peremptory norms, as embodied in VCLT Article 53, 'had been recognized in public international law before the Convention existed, but that instrument gave it both a precision and a substance which made the notion one of its essential provisions'.[16] The representative of France disagreed during the plenary drafting session, expressing his government's opposition to VCLT Article 53 'because it did not agree with the recognition that article gave to *jus cogens*' while another government called *jus cogens* 'still a highly controversial concept which raised the fundamental question of how to recognize the scope and content of a peremptory norm of general international law', noting that time had revealed 'a divergence of views since 1969 regarding the nature of norms of *jus cogens,* which it had not been possible to define'.[17] The text of the Convention was adopted by 67:1, with twenty-three states abstaining; it

[14] See René-Jean Dupuy's remarks at the meeting of the Committee of the Whole on 30 April 1968 (UN Conference on the Law of Treaties, 1st Sess. Vienna, 26 March–24 May 1968, Official Records, Summary records of the plenary meetings of the Committee of the Whole, at 258, para. 74).

[15] First Report of Mr. Dire D. Tladi, Special Rapporteur of the International Law Commission on the topic of *jus cogens*, A/69/10, at 274, para. 3.

[16] According to the Commentary, 'it is apparent from the draft articles that peremptory norms of international law apply to international organizations as well as to states, and this is not surprising'. A/Conf.129/16/Add.1 (vol. II), pp. 39, 44.

[17] United Nations Conference on the Law of Treaties between States and International Organizations or between International Organizations, Vienna, 18 February–21 March 1986, A/Conf.129/16 (vol. I), 17. See also the concerns expressed by Germany, and similar objections raised to Art. 64 which concerns the emergence of a new peremptory norm of general international law (p. 18).

has yet to enter into force. Several states explained their abstention by referring to the articles concerning *jus cogens*, including the dispute settlement provisions on the topic.[18] Even some of those that favoured *jus cogens* expressed uncertainty. The representative of Brazil called *jus cogens* 'a concept in evolution.'[19]

3.2 Definition of *Jus Cogens*

There are many proposed lists of claimed norms *jus cogens*, but the VCLT provides only a cursory and circular means of identification, which falls short of any meaningful definition. According to this, *jus cogens* norms are those accepted and recognized by the international community of states as a whole as ones from which no derogation is permitted. In other words, *jus cogens* norms are *jus cogens* norms. What this formulation does indicate is that it is the attitude of states that determines the issue and that unanimity among them is not required. The ILC, in discussing the first report of its new Special Rapporteur on the topic, agreed that it is the practice of states which gives norms their peremptory character. Further, some ILC members expressed the view that *jus cogens* norms have as their purpose the protection of international public order; yet they still require *opinio juris*, the conviction of the existence of a legal right or obligation of a peremptory nature. The ILC was divided over the issue of whether to provide an illustrative list of *jus cogens* norms.

---

[18] Ibid., pp. 186–194.
[19] Ibid., p. 188.

4

Recent Work of the International Law Commission

4.1 Recent ILC Consideration of the Topic of *Jus Cogens*

Uncertainties over the precise nature of *jus cogens* and its consequences, as well as lack of consensus about which norms fall within this higher category of law led a member of the ILC, Andreas Jacovides, to propose in 1993 the inclusion of *jus cogens* as a possible topic for ILC study. His comment at the time about the lack of relevant standards to determine the legal content of *jus cogens*, or the process by which norms may rise to peremptory status, continue to resonate nearly a quarter of a century after adoption of the VCLT. Nonetheless, the ILC declined to include the topic in the Commission's programme of work at that time, doubting that the proposed study would serve a useful purpose in the absence of relevant State practice and jurisprudence.[1]

In the period since the 1966 draft articles and the 1993 proposal by Mr Jacovides, practice developed rapidly. National and international courts began to refer to *jus cogens* and provide insights about its formation, operation, content, and consequences or effects.[2] States have at times

[1] Already in the 1966 Draft Articles, the Commission noted that the 'view that there is no rule of international law from which States cannot at their own free will contract out has become increasingly difficult to sustain'. See paragraph 1 of the commentary to Draft Article 50 of the 1966 Draft Articles on the Law of Treaties. In paragraph 3 of the commentary to Draft Article 50, the Commission stated that, at that point, it was appropriate to provide for the rule in general terms 'and to leave the full content of this rule to be worked out in State practice and in the jurisprudence of international tribunals'. See Annex A of the Report of the International Law Commission, 69th Sess. (A/69/10) at para. 3.

[2] See, e.g. Military and Paramilitary Activities in and against Nicaragua (*Nicaragua v United States*), ICJ Reports 1986, 14; Arrest Warrant of 11 April 2000 (*DRC v Belgium*) ICJ Reports 2002, 3; Armed Activities on the Territory of the Congo (New Application 2002: *DRC v Rwanda*), ICJ Reports 2006, 99; Jurisdictional Immunities of the State (*Germany v Italy: Greece Intervening*), ICJ Reports 2012, 99. See especially the dissenting opinion of Judge Trindade in the Jurisdictional Immunities of the State case, the joint separate opinions of Judges Higgins,

also referred to *jus cogens* in support of positions that they advance.[3] The Commission itself, in the course of considering other topics, has also made contributions to this development. Article 26 of the Draft Articles on State responsibility, for example, provides that circumstances precluding wrongfulness provided in the draft articles may not be used to justify conduct that is inconsistent with *jus cogens*. The commentary thereto presents a non-exhaustive list of *jus cogens* norms.[4] In addition to repeating the list contained in the commentary to Draft Article 26, the Report of the Study Group on Fragmentation provides a list of 'the most frequently cited candidates' for the status of *jus cogens*.[5] The Commission's Guide to Practice on Reservations to Treaties also provides detailed analysis on the effects of *jus cogens* on the permissibility and consequences of reservations.[6]

Kooijmans, and Buergenthal, and the dissenting opinions of Judges Oda, Al-Khasawneh, and van den Wyngaert in the *Arrest Warrant* case. *Al-Adsani v UK* (Application No. 35763/97), 21 November 2001. See also the separate opinion of Judge ad hoc Lauterpacht in the Application of the Convention on the Prevention and Punishment of the Crime of Genocide (*Bosnia and Herzegovina v Serbia and Montenegro*), ICJ Reports 1993, p. 325 (Separate Opinion of Judge Lauterpacht), paras 100–104 and *Regina v Street Metropolitan Stipendiary Magistrate, ex parte Pinochet Ugarte* (No. 3), 24 March 1999, House of Lords, 119 ILR, p. 136.

[3] See, e.g. statement by Counsel to Belgium in Questions Relating to the Obligation to Prosecute or Extradite (*Belgium v Senegal*), Oral Proceedings, 13 March 2012 (CR 2012/3), para. 3 and statement by Counsel to Senegal in Questions Relating to the Obligation to Prosecute or Extradite (*Belgium v Senegal*), Oral Proceedings, 15 March 2012 (CR 2012/4), para. 39. See also Counter-Memorial of Senegal in Questions Relating to the Obligation to Prosecute or Extradite (*Belgium v Senegal*), para. 51. Similarly, while Germany sought to limit the effects of *jus cogens* in the Jurisdictional Immunities case, its own statement not only did not dispute the existence of *jus cogens* but in fact positively asserted the character of certain norms as *jus cogens*. See, e.g. the Memorial of the Federal Republic of Germany in the *Jurisdiction Immunities* case, 12 June 2009, para. 86 where Germany states: 'Undoubtedly, for instance, *jus cogens* prohibits genocide.' See also Statement of South Africa of 29 October 2009 on the report of the International Law Commission (A/C.6/64/SR.15, paras 69–70) cited in the second report of the Special Rapporteur, Mr Roman Kolodkin on Immunity of State Officials from Foreign Criminal Jurisdiction, 10 June 2010 (A/CN.4/631), para. 9, especially n. 13. On 28 October 2013, during the Sixth Committee's consideration of the report of the International Law Commission, Portugal highlighted *jus cogens* as of 'utmost importance' (A/C.6/68/SR.17), para. 88.

[4] See paragraph 5 of the commentary to Draft Article 26 in which the Commission, in fairly unequivocal terms, states that those 'peremptory norms that are clearly accepted and recognised include the prohibition of aggression, genocide, slavery, racial discrimination, crimes against humanity and torture, and the right to self-determination'.

[5] See paragraph 374 of Report of the Study Group of the International Law Commission on the Fragmentation of International Law: Difficulties Arising from the Diversification and Expansion of International Law, 13 April 2006 (A/CN.4/L.682). See also Conclusion 33 of the Conclusions of the Work of the Study Group on the Fragmentation of International Law: Difficulties Arising from the Diversification and Expansion of International Law (2006).

[6] See, e.g. Commentary to Draft Guide 3.1.5.4 and Guide 4.4.3 of the Guide to Practice on Reservations to Treaties. See also Armed Activities on the Territory of the Congo (New Application 2002: *DRC v Rwanda*) (Separate Opinion of Judge Dugard) (discussing the effect

4.2 The First Report

Despite these developments, it was not until 2015 that the ILC decided to include the topic in its programme of work and appointed South African member Dire Tladi as Special Rapporteur (SR) for the topic.[7] The General Assembly took note of the ILC decision in resolution 70/236 adopted 23 December 2015. At the following session of the ILC, held in 2016, Tladi presented his first report.[8] It set forth his general approach to the topic, and provided a general overview of the issues identified. After consideration at the 2016 session, the Commission referred his draft conclusions in the report to the Drafting Committee, which adopted them provisionally.[9]

The initial report of Tladi addressed conceptual matters such as the nature and definition of *jus cogens* norms.[10] Concerning the methodology, States and the SR agreed that the latter should undertake a thorough analysis of State and judicial practice. Scholarly writings could be used to supplement these sources.

As for the historical antecedents of *jus cogens*, the SR noted that it was literature, going back to the seventeenth century, that recognized the existence of norms from which States could not opt out. He added that State practice was scant, but States had not questioned, during the Vienna Conference, the idea of *jus cogens*, nor its status as part of international law. The SR did not attempt to resolve the theoretical debate concerning the nature of *jus cogens*; instead he proposed three draft conclusions, the first concerning the way in which *jus cogens* rules are to be identified and the legal consequences of that identification. The second draft conclusion states the rule of *jus cogens* may only be modified, derogated from, or abrogated by another rule of *jus cogens*. Finally, the third draft conclusion defines *jus cogens* norms as *jus cogens* norms, that is, as those accepted and recognized by the international community of States as a whole as those from which no derogation, modification, or abrogation is permitted. Significantly, it adds that these norms protect the fundamental values of the international

of reservations that violate *jus cogens*), para. 9. See also Principle 8 of the Guiding Principles applicable to unilateral declarations of States capable of creating legal obligations, with commentaries thereto, Yearbook of the International Law Commission, 2006, vol. II, Part Two.

[7] A/CN.4/693, First Report of Mr Dire Tladi, SR on the topic of *jus cogens*. Annual Report of the ILC, ORGA, 71st Sess., Supp. No. 10, UN Doc. A/71/10.
[8] Ibid.
[9] Ibid.
[10] Ibid.

community and are hierarchically superior to other international law norms and are universally applicable. This suggests that the origins lie in the public policy approach described above.

4.3 The Second Report

At its 69th Session in 2017, the ILC had before it the second report submitted by the SR[11] which aimed to set forth the criteria for the identification of peremptory norms, using the VCLT as a starting point. It was at this session that the ILC decided to change the title of the topic to Peremptory Norms of general international law (*jus cogens*), as the SR had proposed.[12] It also referred to the Drafting Committee draft conclusions 2, 4, 5, 6, and 7.[13] The draft conclusions made little progress in developing criteria for identifying norms *jus cogens*, beyond the statement in the first report that took a positivist approach in referring to recognition and acceptance by the international community of States. Draft conclusion 4 identified two criteria: first, the norm proposed must be a norm of general international law; second, it must be accepted and recognized by the international community of States as a whole as a norm from which no derogation is permitted.

This reiterates the positivist position of the VCLT in its focus on State practice, reinforced in draft conclusion 5, which provides that customary international law is the most common basis for the formation of *jus cogens* norms of international law.[14] General principles of law can also serve as the basis for *jus cogens* norms, while treaties 'may reflect a norm of general international law capable of rising to the level of a *jus cogens* norm of general international law'.[15] This departs somewhat from the jurisprudence of the ICJ, which has looked more favourably to treaty practice.[16]

---

[11] See second report of the SR, Mr Dire Tladi, on *jus cogens*, Doc. A/CN,4/706.

[12] Report of the Commission on the work of its 69th Sess., Official Records of the General Assembly, 72nd Sess., Supp. No. 10 (A/72/10), para. 146. Mr Cissé, however, had suggested that the name of the topic be changed to 'Identification of peremptory norms of international law' (A/CN.4/SR.3373). While Ms Oral agreed with the name change, she stated that the phrase 'general international law' should not be understood as excluding norms under specialized regimes (ibid.).

[13] Report of the Commission on the work of its 69th Sess., Official Records of the General Assembly, 72nd Sess., Suppl. No. 10 (A/72/10), paras 162–210. See also, the Third Report, para. 11.

[14] Draft conclusion 5, para. 1, Second Report (n 13).

[15] Draft conclusion 5, para. 4, ibid.

[16] See section 5.2. For criticism of the report for reducing the value of treaties and general principles of law in the formation of norms *jus cogens*, see the comments of members of

The emphasis on customary international law also clear in the next two draft conclusions, which focus on *opinio juris*, requiring 'an assessment of the opinion of the international community of States as a whole' (draft conclusion 6) and insisting that it is the attitude of States that is relevant; other actors 'may be relevant in providing context and assessing the attitude of States'.[17] Importantly, acceptance and recognition by 'a large majority' of States is sufficient to identify a norm as one of *jus cogens*; universal acceptance and recognition is not needed.[18]

4.4 The Third Report

In 2018, the ILC's 70th Session, the SR delivered his third report,[19] which considered the consequences and legal effects of peremptory norms of general international law. Based on this report, the Commission decided to refer draft conclusions 10 to 23 to the Drafting Committee.[20] In his introduction to this report, the SR noted 'that there was near-universal agreement that customary international law was the most common basis for *jus cogens* norms'.[21] This is a somewhat surprising statement, given that the focus of nearly all the work thus far had been on the impact of peremptory norms on the law of treaties. In fact, much of this report also concerns treaty law, including draft conclusion 13, which addresses the effects of peremptory norms on reservations to treaties, based on earlier work of the ILC and the practice of UN treaty bodies. As for dispute settlement procedures, the SR limits himself to 'encouraging' parties to submit their disputes involving conflict between a treaty and a norm of *jus cogens* to judicial settlement, including the ICJ.[22]

---

the ILC, in particular, Mr Grossman Guiloff (A/CN.4/SR.3370) and Ms Escobar Hernández (A/CN.4/SR.3373); Mr Kolodkin (A/CN.4/SR.3372) and Ms Galvão Teles (A/CN.4/SR.3373). See, for examples of a contrary view, Mr Vásquez-Bermúdez (A/CN.4/SR.3372), Mr Ruda Santolaria (ibid.), and Mr Reinisch (ibid.).

[17] Draft conclusion 7 (n 13), paras 2 and 3.
[18] Draft conclusion 7, para. 3, ibid.
[19] Third report of the SR on peremptory norms of general international law (*jus cogens*), Mr Dire Tladi, Doc. A/CN.4//714 (12 February 2018); Report of the ILC on its 70th sess., Official Records of the General Assembly, 72nd Sess., Supp. No. 10 (A/72/10), para. 146).
[20] Ibid., para. 96.
[21] Ibid., para. 98.
[22] Ibid., para. 101.

Draft conclusion 15 addresses fundamental issues of the relationship between customary international law and *jus cogens* norms. First, based mostly on the decisions of national courts,[23] paragraph 1 asserts that the latter prevail over the former, that is, existing *jus cogens* invalidates conflicting customary rules or prevents them from coming into being. The second paragraph draws inspiration from Article 64 of the VCLT as well as State opinions and judgments of the European Court of Justice. Finally, paragraph 3 insists that the persistent objector rule does not apply to *jus cogens* norms, 'consistent with the universal nature of *jus cogens*', State practice, and the decisions of national and regional courts.[24]

The broad and varied impacts of *jus cogens* norms are further asserted in draft conclusions 16 and 17, which first declare invalid any unilateral act in

---

[23] The notion that customary international law rules that conflict with norms of *jus cogens* are invalid flows from the hierarchical superiority, reflected in the jurisprudence of national and international courts. In *Committee of United States Citizens Living in Nicaragua v Reagan*, the United States Court of Appeals for the District of Columbia observed that *jus cogens* norms 'enjoy the highest status in international law and *prevail over both customary international law* and treaties'. In the United Kingdom, the Queen's Bench Division of the England and Wales High Court of Justice in *R (Mohamed) v Secretary of State for Foreign and Commonwealth Affairs*, also referred to the hierarchical superiority of *jus cogens* norms and, consequently, 'that derogation by States through treaties or rules of customary law not possessing the same status [was] not permitted'. The Argentine Supreme Court has similarly stated that crimes against humanity had the 'character of *jus cogens*, meaning that [the prohibition is] above both treaty law, but above all other sources of international law'. In the *Kenya Section of the International Commission of Jurists v Attorney-General*, the Kenyan High Court stated that *jus cogens* norms 'rendered void any other pre-emptory rules which come into conflict with them'. This sense that norms of *jus cogens* take precedence over other customary international law has also been affirmed in the jurisprudence of regional courts. In *Al-Adsani*, for example, the ECtHR determined that *jus cogens* norms are those norms that enjoy 'a higher rank in the international hierarchy than treaty law and even "ordinary" customary rules'. *Al-Adsani v United Kingdom*, joint dissenting opinion of Judges Rozakis and Caflisch (joined by Judges Wildhaber, Costa, Cabral Barreto, and Vajić), para. 1. *Al-Adsani v United Kingdom*, joint dissenting opinion of Judges Rozakis and Caflisch (joined by Judges Wildhaber, Costa, Cabral Barreto, and Vajić), para. 1. Furthermore, in *Belhas et al. v Moshe Ya'Alon*, the United States Court of Appeals for the District of Columbia described *jus cogens* norms as 'norms so universally accepted that *all States* are deemed to be bound by them under international law'. Furthermore, in *Belhas et al. v Moshe Ya'Alon*, the United States Court of Appeals for the District of Columbia described *jus cogens* norms as 'norms so universally accepted that *all States* are deemed to be bound by them under international law'. United States, *Belhas et al. v Moshe Ya'Alon*, 515 F.3d 1279 (DC Cir. 2008), at 1291–1292 (emphasis added). The IACtHR has similarly concluded that norms of *jus cogens* 'bind all States'. Advisory Opinion OC-18/03 of 17 September 2003 on the juridical condition and rights of undocumented migrants, requested by the United Mexican States, Ser. A, No. 18, paras 4–5. See also written statement of 19 June 1995 by the Government of Mexico on the request for an advisory opinion submitted to the International Court of Justice by the General Assembly at its 49th Sess. (resolution 49/75K), para. 7 ('The norms … are of a legally binding nature for all the States (*jus cogens*)'). See also Iran (Islamic Republic of) (A/C.6/68/SR.26), para. 4 ('the "persistent objector", had no place in the formation of *jus cogens*').

[24] Ibid., para. 102.

conflict with a norm of *jus cogens* and then asserts that resolutions of inter-governmental organizations do not create obligations for States if they conflict with a norm of *jus cogens*.[25] This proposed conclusion, according to the SR, is supported by 'a significant amount of literature and public statements of States',[26] as well as by decisions of domestic, regional, and international courts. To the extent possible such resolutions should be interpreted in a manner consistent with *jus cogens* norms.

Draft conclusion 18 is said to reflect virtually universal agreement that *jus cogens* norms also establish *erga omnes* obligations.[27] The remaining draft conclusions address State responsibility and *jus cogens* norms. Paragraph 1 of Draft conclusion 19 confirms that the circumstances precluding wrongfulness in the articles on State responsibility do not apply to breaches of obligations arising from *jus cogens* norms. Draft conclusion 20 concerns an asserted duty to cooperate to bring to an end, by lawful means, any serious breach of a *jus cogens* norm, defined as a breach that is either gross or systematic. The SR finds support for this 'well-established principle of international law' in the *Wall* Advisory Opinion[28] of the ICJ as well as the *La Cantuta* case[29] decided by the Inter-American Court of Human Rights (IACtHR).

Draft conclusion 20 continues in this vein, setting forth a duty not to recognize as lawful a situation created by breach of a *jus cogens* norm and a duty not to aid or assist in maintaining such a situation,[30] as previously affirmed by the ILC in the articles on State responsibility[31] and the ICJ in the *Namibia*[32] and the *Wall* advisory opinions, as well as in UN resolutions. Unlike draft conclusion 20, these duties apply even to breaches not deemed 'serious', because the duty of non-recognition arises based on the violation of a peremptory norm and neither of the cited ICJ opinions had specified seriousness as a requisite to the duty not to recognize or assist in a *jus cogens*

---

[25] Ibid., paras 103–104.

[26] Ibid., para. 104.

[27] Ibid., para. 105.

[28] Legal Consequences of the Construction of a Wall in the Occupied Palestinian Territory, Advisory Opinion, ICJ Reports 2004, p. 136, at p. 200, para. 159.

[29] *La Cantuta v Peru* (Merits, Reparations, and Costs) Series C, No. 162, Judgment, 29 November 2006, IACtHR, para. 160.

[30] Report of the ILC on its 70th sess. (n 19), para. 107.

[31] *Yearbook ... 2001*, vol. II (Part Two) and corrigendum, para. 76.

[32] Legal Consequences for States of the Continued Presence of South Africa in Namibia (South West Africa) notwithstanding Security Council Resolution 276 (1970) Advisory Opinion, ICJ Reports 1971, p. 16 at p. 54, para. 119.

violation. Also, the duty of non-recognition did not require positive action, warranting the lower threshold.

The remaining draft conclusions deal with crimes prohibited by *jus cogens* norms, based on the ILC draft articles on crimes against humanity.[33] The first of the draft conclusions in this section, number 23, concerns jurisdiction based on nationality, territory, or universality, although it is acknowledged that the practice in this regard is not settled. The final draft conclusion concerns the lack of immunity for commission of *jus cogens* crimes. The report notes the criticism and conflicting State practice on this issue, but points out that the conflicting cases are typically based on civil proceedings and those brought against States. They are not meant to serve as precedents for immunities in a criminal context, as reflected in the ICJ judgment in the *Jurisdictional Immunities of the State (Germany v Italy, Greece intervening)* case.[34]

The third report went well beyond the law of treaties and State responsibility, in looking at the consequences of peremptory norms for States in respect to international criminal law, customary international law, and the law of international organizations, all of which have generated divergent views in the literature, and concern for the practice problems that may arise.[35] The debate in the ILC also revealed considerable caution. Several members referred to the dearth of relevant State practice and the complexity of the issues involved.[36] As much as possible, these members sought to have the results of this study reflect existing law and established practice, especially in regard to the consequences of *jus cogens* on other sources of international law.[37] Specific issues were raised about the Rapporteur's proposal to eliminate the possibility of being a persistent objector to a rule of *jus cogens* emerging from customary international law. Some members felt the proposal did not reflect the complexity of the relationship between the superior status of *jus cogens* norms and the principle of State consent.[38] One key question concerned the appropriate result if a persistent objector should raise objections before a norm is recognized as a *jus cogens* norm, being expressed during the formative period.[39]

---

[33] Official Records of the General Assembly, 72nd Sess., Supp. No. 10 (A/72/10), para. 45.
[34] *Jurisdictional Immunities of the State (Germany v Italy, Greece intervening)*, Judgment, ICJ Reports 2012, p. 99, 130, and 141, paras 70 and 96.
[35] Report of the ILC on its 70th sess. (n 19), para. 111.
[36] Ibid., para. 112.
[37] Ibid.
[38] Ibid., para. 128.
[39] Ibid., para. 129.

Another issue of concern was the reference to the Security Council in draft conclusion 17. Some members objected to singling out the Council, while other members felt it was important to do so, given the unique powers and legal consequences for States of the resolutions adopted under Chapter VII of the UN Charter as well the impact of Article 103.[40]

Draft conclusions 22 and 23 also provoked conflicting views about the advisability of addressing individual criminal responsibility and immunity.[41] Some members objected, considering it beyond the scope of the project, while others expressed support for including the topics. Members were particularly concerned about the lack of national legislation or case law on prosecuting *jus cogens* violations committed on a State's territory or by a State's national. They claimed the lack of State practice provided no support for the draft conclusion; the same point was made about the asserted duty to exercise universal jurisdiction. Some suggested adding a 'without prejudice' clause or the phrase 'in accordance with international law'.[42] There were more objections to these final draft conclusions, again based on the argument that State practice does not support them. The SR admitted that the relative dearth of State practice presented a challenge, but he felt it was not an insurmountable obstacle, because the Commission could faithfully assess the practice, together with other reliable sources, to come to the most accurate description of existing international law. As the SR observed in his subsequent fourth report, there were some sharply critical comments on the 'complicated and sensitive' issues discussed in the third report.[43] The States in the Sixth Committee were also divided in their reactions to the third report.[44]

---

[40] Ibid., paras 131–133.

[41] Ibid., paras 141–148.

[42] Ibid.

[43] Fourth report on peremptory norms of general international law (*jus cogens*) by Dire Tladi, Special Rapporteur, International Law Commission 71st Sess., Geneva, 29 April–7 June and 8 July–9 August 2019 (A/CN.4/727) 31 January 2019, para. 5, n. 7. Mr Tladi noted that strongly critical statements were made by Mr Zagaynov (A/CN.4/SR.3416); Mr Murphy (A/CN.4/SR.3416); Mr Rajput (A/CN.4/SR.3418); Mr Huang (A/CN.4/SR.3419); Sir Michael Wood (A/CN.4/SR.3421); and Mr Valencia-Ospina (A/CN.4/SR.3421). However, unlike other critical members, Mr Valencia-Ospina's criticism was not that the SR went too far, but, on the contrary, that he did not go far enough. The SR added that Mr Nolte (A/CN.4/SR.3417), while generally critical, was not as severe as the others.

[44] Of the States that commented on the topic, the following were generally negative: China (A/C.6/73/SR.25); France (A/C.6/73/SR.26); Romania (ibid.); Israel (A/C.6/73/SR.27); Turkey (ibid.); and the United States of America (A/C.6/73/SR.29). States that adopted an overall positive stance were: Bahamas, on behalf of the Caribbean Community (CARICOM) (A/C.6/73/SR.20); Austria (statement of 26 October 2018; see also A/C.6/73/SR.25); Brazil (A/C.6/73/SR.25); Cyprus (ibid.); Egypt (ibid.); Mexico (ibid.); Singapore (statement of 30 October 2018; see also A/C.6/73/SR.25); Estonia (A/C.6/73/SR.26); Japan (ibid.); New Zealand (ibid.);

4.5 The Fourth Report

The fourth report, presented in 2019,[45] dealt with the question of the existence of regional *jus cogens* and the contentious issue of whether or not to
include an illustrative list in the conclusions to the study, based on norms
previously recognized by the Commission as possessing a peremptory
character. The Commission debated these two matters, then adopted on
first reading, 23 draft conclusions and a draft annex, together with commentaries thereto, on peremptory norms of general international law (*jus
cogens*). These were meant to be transmitted through the UN Secretary
General to governments for comments and observations.

The illustrative list is especially noteworthy, identifying norms the ILC
has previously labelled as peremptory in character; most of them are also
recognized as violations of international criminal law. They are: the prohibitions of aggression, torture, genocide, crimes against humanity, apartheid
and racial discrimination, and slavery. To these, the SR added the right of
self-determination and the basic rules of humanitarian law.

In the fourth report, the SR responded to several criticisms raised
by delegations in the Sixth Committee to his work. One methodological
issue raised by several delegations concerned the importance of practice in
the consideration of the topic. A number of States questioned the Special
Rapporteur's reliance on theory and doctrine rather than State practice.[46]
The Rapporteur 'noted that, although a few States made this assertion, this
was not the majority view and, in fact, some States explicitly observed that

---

Portugal (ibid.); Thailand (ibid.); Greece (A/C.6/73/SR.27 and statement of 30 October 2018);
Islamic Republic of Iran (A/C.6/73/SR.27); Malaysia (statement of 30 October 2018; see also
A/C.6/73/SR.27); Republic of Korea (A/C.6/73/SR.27 and statement of 30 October 2018).

[45] Fourth Report (n 43).

[46] Czech Republic (A/C.6/73/SR.25) ('the Special Rapporteur's approach was based primarily on references to doctrine rather than to international practice'); France (A/C.6/73/
SR.26); Romania (ibid.) ('The Commission's consideration of the topic must be based on State
practice, rather than on doctrinal approaches'); Slovakia (ibid.) ('Slovakia noted with concern
that several of the draft conclusions on the topic proposed by the SR were based merely on
doctrinal opinions rather than State practice'); and Israel (A/C.6/73/SR.27 and statement of 30
October 2018) (which had a number of concerns regarding the methodology employed by the
SR, including that 'the Special Rapporteur had relied too much on theory and doctrine, rather
than on relevant State practice'). See also United States (A/C.6/73/SR.29) ('More generally, the
lack of State practice or jurisprudence on the bulk of the questions addressed in the project had
clear implications for the role and function of any draft conclusions ultimately adopted on the
topic. Although framed as "draft conclusions", the statements contained in the project were not
grounded in legal authority, but rather reflected an effort to imagine, through deductive reasoning, ways in which certain principles could apply in hypothetical circumstances.').

the Special Rapporteur's third report relied on State practice, notwith-standing the dearth thereof'.[47] He responded that it was difficult to answer the criticism that the work followed a theoretical approach and had not relied on practice, 'since none of the States have pointed to a single draft conclusion entirely unsupported by practice. Not a single draft conclusion proposed in the third report (or for that matter any of the previous reports) is based solely on doctrine'.[48] Despite the small minority of States that made this allegation, he found it 'so serious and damning that' he felt it neces-sary to give some examples to refute it. State practice in the form of na-tional judicial decisions, statements by States, treaty practice, resolutions of the General Assembly,[49] and resolutions of the Security Council[50] was provided in the third report. The report also contains invocations of inter-national and regional jurisprudence.[51] He concluded his defence by saying that 'It suffices to say that much of the work in the third report is based on the 1969 Vienna Convention'.[52]

a. The question of regional *jus cogens*

States have long been concerned about how the Commission would, even-tually, address the issue of regional *jus cogens*.[53] During the debate on the Commission's report in 2018, several States commented on the matter and debated whether regional peremptory norms could exist. Malaysia, for ex-ample, noted that the concept of regional *jus cogens* 'might ... create con-fusion and should therefore be avoided'.[54] The United Kingdom said it was 'doubtful as to the utility of considering "regional" *jus cogens*'.[55] In its

[47] Fourth Report (n 43), para. 16.

[48] Ibid.

[49] See the third report for references to General Assembly resolution 33/28 A of 7 December 1979 and General Assembly resolution 3411 D of 28 November 1975.

[50] See the third report for references to Security Council resolution 353 (1974); 241 and Security Council resolution 276 (1970).

[51] See the third report for references to *Prosecutor v Taylor* (Special Court for Sierra Leone); *Armed Activities on the Territory of the Congo* (judgment of the International Court of Justice); *Council of the European Union v Front populaire pour la libération de la sauguiael-hamra et du rio de oro (Front Polisario)*; and the *Oil Platforms* case (ICJ).

[52] He claimed that the work of the third report was based on the VCLT, Fourth Report (n 43), at n. 31.

[53] K. Gastorn, 2017, 'Defining the imprecise contours of *jus cogens* in international law', 16 *Chinese J. Int'l Law*, 643–662, at 659–660.

[54] Malaysia (A/C.6/73/SR.27).

[55] United Kingdom (statement of 30 October 2018; see also A/C.6/73/SR.27).

statement, Thailand indicated that it was of the view that 'that the accept-ance of the existence of regional *jus cogens* would contradict and under-mine the notion of *jus cogens* being norms "accepted and recognized by the international community of States as a whole" and therefore would not be possible under international law'.[56] Similarly, Finland, on behalf of the Nordic countries, said it was 'unconvinced about the possibility of recon-ciling regional *jus cogens* with the notion of *jus cogens* as peremptory norms of general international law'.[57] Greece stated that it firmly believed that the idea of regional *jus cogens* 'ran contrary to the very notion of *jus cogens*, which was by definition universal'.[58] Similarly, South Africa said that it was 'concerned that entertaining a concept such as regional *jus cogens* would have a watering-down effect on the supreme and universal nature of *jus cogens*'.[59] The United States, for its part, 'questioned the utility of consid-ering "regional *jus cogens*" and agreed with other delegations that that con-cept appeared to be at variance with the view that *jus cogens* norms were "accepted and recognized by the international community as a whole" '.[60] Portugal, which stated that it may be 'an appealing exercise from the intel-lectual point of view' to study the issue of regional *jus cogens,* urged some caution because the 'integrity of peremptory norms of general international law as norms that are universally recognizable and applicable should not be jeopardized'.[61]

While acknowledging that there are writers who have supported the no-tion of regional *jus cogens,*[62] the SR argued that there are several problems with the concept. The first problem concerns the lack of practice to sub-stantiate the existence of regional *jus cogens.*[63] The second addresses a the-oretical concern central to the objections of States about the establishment or formation of regional *jus cogens.* The SR found it difficult to explain why an individual State in a region, perhaps one hostile to that State, would be

---

[56] Thailand (A/C.6/73/SR.26).
[57] Finland (on behalf of the Nordic countries) (A/C.6/73/SR.24).
[58] Greece (A/C.6/73/SR.27).
[59] South Africa (A/C.6/73/SR.27).
[60] United States (A/C.6/73/SR.29).
[61] Portugal (statement of 26 October 2018 and A/C.6/73/SR.26).
[62] He cites in particular R. Kolb, 2015, *Peremptory International Law (Jus Cogens): A General Inventory* (Oxford, Hart), especially at pp. 97 ff.; E. de Wet, 2006, 'The emergence of inter-national and regional value systems as a manifestation of the emerging international constitu-tional order', *19 Leiden J. Int'l Law*, 611–632, at 617 (positing that the European Convention on Human Rights and Fundamental Freedoms has arguably become regional *jus cogens*); and G.I. Tunkin, 1965, *Theory of International Law* (Paris, Pedone), p. 444.
[63] Fourth Report (n 43), at para. 26.

bound to a norm that is not universal *jus cogens* and to which it has not consented, or if it has consented, it has not agreed with its peremptory status.[64] The rationale for the exceptional power of *jus cogens* to bind *sans* consent can be found in the fact that these norms are so fundamental to the international community that derogation from them cannot be permitted.[65]

The Commission has accepted the possibility of regional customary international law or 'particular customary international law'.[66] The question is whether the same doctrinal reasoning that allows regional customary international law does not, similarly, allow for the possibility of regional *jus cogens*. He asserts that the answer must be no because, while regional customary international law must be subject to the persistent objector rule (at least, if general customary international law is), this cannot be the case for regional *jus cogens*, otherwise it would cease to be peremptory.[67]

Another conceptual difficulty relates to the question of definition of 'region'. Universal application is easily defined as all States. Regional *jus cogens*, as a matter of law, is, however, problematic to define. The boundaries of Europe, for example, or Asia, or the Americas are uncertain. They each have components that can vary in number, depending on the context. Normally, these rest on agreement of the States in the region, for a specific purpose.[68] Thus, for example, the Southern African region means different things in the African Union and in the United Nations. In the light of this uncertainty, the concept of regional *jus cogens* would create the conceptual and practical difficulty of knowing which States were bound by a particular norm asserted to be regional *jus cogens*.

Third, and linked to the above difficulty, it is not clear whether regional *jus cogens* must be linked to an existing regional treaty regime. The examples given to assert regional *jus cogens* relate either to the protection of human rights in Europe or the Inter-American human rights system.[69] Yet, as treaty systems based on the agreement of the parties to those regional systems, it is unclear to what extent those could generate norms of *jus cogens*.[70] This does not exclude the possibility that these regional treaty norms could lead to the evolution of universal norms of *jus cogens* such as the prohibition

---

[64] Ibid., para. 28.

[65] Ibid.

[66] See draft conclusion 16 of the draft conclusions on the identification of customary international law, adopted by the Commission on second reading, A/73/10, para. 65, at p. 154.

[67] Fourth Report (n 43), at para. 28.

[68] Ibid., para. 29.

[69] Ibid., para. 30.

[70] See, for discussion, the Special Rapporteur's second report (A/CN.4/706), paras 53–59.

of enforced disappearance, the origins of which are from the region of the Americas, but shows how a customary norm can evolve to one of *jus cogens*.[71] While the Inter-American System through the Commission and the Court have more readily found the existence of norms of *jus cogens*,[72] this is different from the notion of regional *jus cogens*. The Inter-American Court and Commission have been quite open to recognizing norms of *jus cogens*, but those norms of *jus cogens* have not been characterized as regional *jus cogens*. Indeed, the Inter-American human rights system provides no support for the notion of regional *jus cogens*.

In contrast to the analysis of the SR, some authors have argued that regional *jus cogens* is a useful counter to the so-called European-based system of international law.[73] Using the Inter-American System for the protection of human rights as a source of case law, they examine its more comprehensive list of *jus cogens* norms. They conclude that it offers a counter-hegemonic basis for constructing or recognizing international norms of a peremptory character.[74] The authors cite Article 27(2) of the American Convention as an example of regional non-derogability, an attribute of *jus cogens*.[75] To this treaty, the role of the Inter-American Court has added its interpretive rulings in cases and advisory opinions. According to former judge and now ICJ Judge Antonio Cançado Trindade, it has been this Court that has contributed the most to the development of the concept and norms of *jus cogens*.[76] He correctly notes that the Court first pronounced any form of discrimination and denial of equality as well as the prohibition of enforced disappearances as acts banned by *jus cogens* norms; importantly, the latter, due to its importance and the nature of the rights involved, imposes

---

[71] Ibid., para. 30.

[72] See section 5.2 (nn 144–147).

[73] T. de A.F.R. Cardoso Squeff and M. de Almeida Rosa, 2018, 'Jus Cogens: An European concept? An emancipatory conceptual review from the inter-American system of human rights', *15 Brazilian J. Int'l L.*, 124–137.

[74] F. Frizzo Bragato, 2014, 'Para além do discurso eurocêntrico dos dereito humanos: Contribuções da descolonialidade', *19 Revista novos estudos juridicos*, 201–230.

[75] Art. 27(2) specifies a longer list of such rights than does either the ICCPR, Art. 4, or the European Convention on Human Rights (ECHR), Art. 4. The ACHR lists as non-derogable the right to legal personality (Art. 3); the right to life (Art. 4); the right to humane treatment and freedom from torture (Art. 5); prohibition of slavery and servitude (Art. 6); principle of legality and non-retroactivity of law (Art. 9); freedom of conscience and religion (Art. 12); protection of the family (Art. 17); right to a name (Art. 18); rights of the child (Art. 19); right to a nationality (Art. 20); and political rights (Art. 23).

[76] A.A. Cançado Trindade, 2013, *El Ejercicio de la funcion judicial internacional: Memorias de la Corte Interamericano de Derecho Humanos* (3rd edn, Belo Horizonte, Brazil, Del Rey Publications), p. 75.

on the State implicated the duty to investigate and identify the perpetrators, try them, and impose appropriate punishment upon their convictions.[77] The assertion of regional human rights *jus cogens* is based on the idea of a common identity forged by membership in a common community and the special nature of the rules that bind such a common community, but *jus cogens* norms must meet particular requirements, as defined in the second report of the Special Rapporteur, and for which particular consequences ensue.[78]

Finally, it should be recalled that *jus cogens* is exceptional. In general, as a rule, norms of international law are derogable and can be modified freely through the exercise of sovereignty.[79] To the extent that norms of regional law flow from the free exercise of the will of States to constrain their sovereignty, these are not norms of *jus cogens* properly so called. Such rules are similar to non-derogable provisions in treaties that do not constitute *jus cogens*, at least not in the manner understood in the 1969 Vienna Convention.[80]

From a conceptual (and practical) perspective, the greatest difficulty for the notion of regional *jus cogens* relates not so much to the formation of norms of regional *jus cogens* but to the consequences that should follow from such norms.[81] The SR discussed the consequences of *jus cogens* identified in his third report,[82] noting that no major issues were raised concerning the substance of the draft conclusions he proposed. He especially identifies the difficulty, given the absence of practice, of envisaging how the consequences of universal *jus cogens* might be given effect in vis-a-vis regional

---

[77] IACtHR, Case of Goiburú and Others (Merits, Reparations, and Costs), Judgment of 22 September 2006, Ser. C, No. 153.

[78] Fourth Report (n 43), at para. 32.

[79] *North Sea Continental Shelf*, Judgment, ICJ Reports 1969, p. 3 at p. 42, para. 72 ('Without attempting to enter into, still less pronounce upon any question of *jus cogens*, it is well understood that, in practice, rules of international law can, by agreement, be derogated from in particular cases, or as between particular parties'); *South West Africa, Second Phase*, ICJ Reports 1966, p. 6, dissenting opinion of Judge Tanaka, p. 298 ('*jus cogens*, recently examined by the International Law Commission, [is] a kind of imperative law which constitutes the contrast to the *jus dispositivum*, capable of being changed by way of agreement between States').

[80] An example is given of Article 20 of the Covenant of the League of Nations which provides, first, that the Covenant abrogates all obligations inconsistent with its terms, and, second, that members 'will not enter into any engagements inconsistent' with the terms of the Covenant. This, being a treaty rule, applicable only to members and subject to amendment and even abrogation by any later agreement, Article 20 cannot be seen as an example of peremptoriness in a significant way. Covenant of the League of Nations (Versailles, 28 April 1919), League of Nations, Official Journal, No. 1, February 1920, p. 3.

[81] Fourth Report (n 43), at para. 33.

[82] Ibid., paras 33–37.

jus cogens. He concludes that the existence of a common set of unifying and binding norms in different regions does not translate into a recognition of regional *jus cogens*; it is simply a reflection of the general structure of international law that allows States to have particular rules that are different and distinct from general rules of international law.[83]

b. Whether to include an illustrative list of *jus cogens* norms

During the Commission's consideration of the Special Rapporteur's first report, some ILC members expressed doubt about the elaboration of an illustrative list,[84] while many others expressed support for such a course.[85] During the consideration of the second report, ILC members who had been newly elected to the Commission and other members who had not had the opportunity to express their views on the issue of an illustrative list stated their preferences. Many of these members expressed support for the illustrative list.[86] There were also suggestions for some kind of middle ground.[87]

The difference of views within the Commission on whether an illustrative list should be elaborated was echoed in the divergent opinions of States. Many States expressed their views during the debate in the Sixth Committee on the report of the Commission at its sixty-sixth session. A slight majority of the States that spoke supported the elaboration of an illustrative list.[88]

---

[83] Ibid.

[84] Members opposed to or expressing doubt about the illustrative list were: Sir Michael Wood (A/CN.4/SR.3314); Mr Nolte (A/CN.4/SR.3315); and Mr Murphy (A/CN.4/SR.3316).

[85] See first report (A/CN.4/693), para. 9.

[86] Members supporting an illustrative list were: Mr Murase (A/CN.4/SR.3314); Mr Caflisch (ibid.); Mr Kittichaisaree (A/CN.4/SR.3315); Mr Park (A/CN.4/SR.3316); Mr Saboia (ibid.); Mr Candioti (A/CN.4/SR.3317); Mr Forteau (ibid.); Mr Vásquez-Bermúdez (A/CN.4/SR.3322); Ms Escobar Hernández (ibid.); and Mr Niehaus (A/CN.4/SR.3323).

[87] For example, Mr Hassouna suggested that an indirect illustrative list could be provided in the commentaries (A/CN.4/SR.3315), a view supported by Ms Lehto (A/CN.4/SR.3372) and Mr Ouazzani Chahdi (A/CN.4/SR.3373). This view was adopted by Mr Nolte (A/CN.4/SR.3315) during the consideration of the second report of the SR.

[88] Brazil (A/C.6/73/SR.25) ('It would be useful to find a creative way of elaborating an illustrative list of *jus cogens* norms while respecting the understanding that the Commission should be discussing process and method, as opposed to the content of the peremptory norms.'); New Zealand (A/C.6/73/SR.26); Portugal (ibid.) ('an illustrative list would not impair the progressive development of *jus cogens*. However, it was likely that a debate on that list would be time-consuming and complex'); and Slovakia (ibid.) ('His delegation was open-minded about the elaboration of an illustrative list of peremptory norms and its future inclusion in the outcome of the topic. If such a list was not included in the text itself, it might be useful to mention in the commentary.')

States also made their views known during the consideration by the Sixth Committee of the Commission's 2018 report. Again, as in the Commission, some States supported the inclusion of an illustrative list[89] while other States were opposed to it.[90]

Members of the Commission and States that supported the elaboration of an illustrative list gave two reasons for its inclusion. The main reason was its utility and value for identifying norms that already meet the criteria for *jus cogens*. Secondly, elaboration of an illustrative list would demonstrate how to apply the criteria to identify *jus cogens* developed by the Commission. Those who opposed the elaboration of a list mounted several arguments. First, they claimed that a list, no matter how carefully it was elaborated, would create the impression of excluding other norms.[91] This was also the main reason advanced for excluding a list during the drafting of the 1966 articles on the law of treaties, although reference was made to some norms as having that character in the commentary.[92] Second, it was claimed that elaborating an illustrative list would be inordinately difficult. As early as his second report, the SR asked members of the Commission to comment on the issue and expressed his own uncertainty about it.

The SR noted that the Commission had previously identified *jus cogens* norms in other studies and reports. The report of the Study Group on 'Fragmentation of international law: difficulties arising from diversification and expansion of international law' identified the following as 'the most frequently cited candidates for the status of *jus cogens*': the prohibition of 'aggressive use of force', the right of self-defence, the prohibition of genocide, the prohibition of torture, crimes against humanity, the prohibition of slavery and the slave trade, the prohibition of piracy, the prohibition of 'racial discrimination and *apartheid*', and the prohibition of 'hostilities directed at civilian population ("basic rules of international humanitarian

---

[89] Austria (A/C.6/73/SR.25); Cyprus (ibid.); Japan (A/C.6/73/SR.26); and Republic of Korea (A/C.6/73/SR.27).

[90] Finland (on behalf of the Nordic countries) (A/C.6/73/SR.24); Germany (A/C.6/73/SR.26); Netherlands (ibid.); Thailand (ibid.); Israel (A/C.6/73/SR.27); South Africa (ibid.); and Sudan (A/C.6/73/SR.28).

[91] Para. (3) of the commentary to Draft Article 50 of the draft articles on the law of treaties, *Yearbook ... 1966*, vol. II ('the mention of some cases of treaties void for conflict with a rule of *jus cogens* might, even with the most careful drafting, lead to misunderstanding as to the position concerning other cases not mentioned in the article').

[92] It seems that the Commission, in 1966, may have believed all the norms mentioned in the commentary to be *jus cogens*. In the commentary to the articles on State responsibility, the Commission seems to indicate that all the norms in the 1966 draft articles constitute a list of what the Commission accepted as having attained the status of *jus cogens*.

law")'.[93] The list in the conclusions of the Study Group differs from this in that the report referred to 'self-defence' but the conclusions did not.[94] In its place, the conclusions referred to the right of self-determination, something not included in the 2006 report of the Study Group.[95]

In the articles on State responsibility, the Commission also provided examples of the most frequently cited norms of *jus cogens*.[96] In the commentary to Article 26, the Commission identified the 'norms that are clearly accepted and recognized' as *jus cogens*: 'the prohibitions of aggression, genocide, slavery, racial discrimination, crimes against humanity and torture, and the right to self-determination'.[97]

The commentary to Article 40 of the articles on State responsibility also contained a list of *jus cogens* norms, seemingly based on the commentary to Article 50 of the draft articles on the law of treaties of 1966. First, consistent with paragraph (1) of the commentary to the 1966 draft articles, it refers to the prohibition of aggression[98] or 'the law of the Charter concerning the prohibition of the use of force'. Second, the norms referred to in paragraph (3) of the commentary to Article 50 of the 1966 draft articles are cited as norms that had achieved status of *jus cogens*, i.e. 'the prohibitions against slavery and the slave trade, genocide, and racial discrimination and apartheid'.[99] Although the commentary to Draft Article 50 in the 1966 draft

---

[93] See 'Fragmentation of international law: difficulties arising from the diversification and expansion of international law', report of the Study Group of the International Law Commission finalized by Martti Koskenniemi (A/CN.4/L.682 and Corr.1 and Add.1) (available on the Commission's website, documents of the 58th Sess.; the final text will be published as an addendum to *Yearbook ... 2006*, vol. II (Part One)), para. 374.

[94] See conclusions of the work of the Study Group on fragmentation of international law, *Yearbook ... 2006*, vol II (Part II), para. 251, at para. (33).

[95] Ibid. The reference to aggressive force rather than just 'the use of force' indicates that the right to use force in self-defence is part of the *jus cogens* norm.

[96] M. den Heijer and H. van der Wilt, 2015, 'Jus cogens and the humanization and fragmentation of international law', *46 Neth. Yearb. Int'l Law*, 3–21, at 9, describing the *jus cogens* status of the norms in the articles. on State responsibility as 'beyond contestation'. See also J.E. Christófolo, 2016, *Solving Antinomies between Peremptory Norms in Public International Law* (Geneva, Schulthess), pp. 151–152; and T. Weatherall, 2015, *Jus cogens: International Law and Social Contract* (Cambridge, Cambridge University Press), p. 202.

[97] See para. (5) of the commentary to Art. 26 of the articles on State responsibility, *Yearbook .... 2001*, vol. II (Part Two) and corrigendum, paras 76–77, at p. 85.

[98] Ibid. 'There also seems to be widespread agreement with other examples listed in the Commission's commentary to draft article 50 (subsequently adopted as article 53 of the 1969 Vienna Convention): *viz.* the prohibitions against slavery and the slave trade, genocide, and racial discrimination and apartheid. These practices have been prohibited in widely ratified international treaties and conventions admitting of no exception.'

[99] Ibid.

articles was ambiguous as to the status of these norms, the commentary to Article 40 is clear about their status as *jus cogens*.[100]

In addition to those norms, the commentary to Draft Article 40 identified a few other norms as *jus cogens*.[101] These are: the prohibition against torture, as defined in the Convention against Torture and Other Cruel, Inhuman or Degrading Treatment or Punishment,[102] the basic rules of international humanitarian law applicable in armed conflict, and 'the obligation to respect the right of self-determination'.[103]

In sum, the Commission generally agreed that norms of *jus cogens* are few in number.[104] Further, the Commission has been fairly consistent that the following norms have attained the status of *jus cogens*:

- the prohibition of aggression or aggressive force, i.e., 'the law of the Charter concerning the prohibition of the use of force');
- the prohibition of genocide;
- the prohibition of slavery;
- the prohibition of apartheid and racial discrimination;
- the prohibition of crimes against humanity;
- the prohibition of torture;
- the right to self-determination; and
- the basic rules of international humanitarian law.

Although the SR claimed that this list is accepted by States as well as writers,[105] he examined State practice and the jurisprudence of international courts and tribunals to determine whether the peremptory character of those norms is 'accepted and recognized by the international community of States as a whole'. The following chapters will to do so as well.

---

[100] Ibid.

[101] Para. (5) of the commentary to Art. 40 (n 97), at p. 113.

[102] Convention against Torture and Other Cruel, Inhuman or Degrading Punishment or Treatment (New York, 10 December 1984), UN, *Treaty Series*, vol. 1465, No. 24841, at 85.

[103] Para. (5) of the commentary to Art. 40 (n 97), at p. 113.

[104] Para. (2) of the commentary to Draft Art. 50 of the draft articles on the law of treaties, *Yearbook ... 1966*, vol. II, ch. II, s. C, at 248 ('Moreover, the majority of the general rules of international law do not have that character').

[105] One notable exception was Israel (A/C.6/73/SR.27), which questioned whether the right to self-determination was a norm of *jus cogens*.

5

State Practice*

The recent ILC work on *jus cogens*, especially in response to comments and critiques from States, paid great attention to State practice supporting the draft conclusions of the Special Rapporteur. Indeed, as much as possible, the SR and the ILC as a whole rooted their findings and recommendations in an extensive citation of precedents. The invocation of practice was broadly inclusive, ranging from votes and official statements in international organizations, through treaty practice (including general comments and conclusions of treaty bodies), to international and national jurisprudence. This approach lends strength to the ILC work.

5.1 Treaty Practice, Votes, and Official Statements in International Organizations

As a matter of treaty practice, the criminalization of genocide can be found not only in the 1951 Genocide Convention, but also in the Rome Statute of the International Criminal Court,[1] and the Malabo Protocol to the Statute of the African Court.[2] Though not treaties, the Statutes of the International Tribunal for the Former Yugoslavia and the International Tribunal for Rwanda also criminalize in absolute terms acts of genocide.[3] None of those instruments provide any possibility for derogation. While grounds for excluding responsibility may be provided, these are not derogations but affect

---

* This chapter draws upon materials published in: Dinah Shelton, 'Sherlock Holmes and the mystery of jus cogens', 46 Netherlands Yearbook of International Law, (2015) 23–50. Reprinted with permission. Dinah Shelton, 'International Law and "Relative Normativity'" in M.D Evans (ed.), International Law, (4th edn, OUP 2014) 137–166.
[1] Rome Statute of the Rape and other forms of sexual violence have long been prohibited by international humanitarian law, as the International Criminal Court (ICC) has affirmed International Criminal Court (Rome, 17 July 1998), United Nations, *Treaty Series*, vol. 2187, No. 38544, p. 3, Art. 6.
[2] Protocol on Amendments to the Protocol on the Statute of the African Court of Justice and Human Rights (Malabo, 27 June 2014), available from www.au.int, annex, Art. 28(b).
[3] Statute of the International Tribunal for the Former Yugoslavia, S/25704, annex, Art. 4; statute of the International Tribunal for Rwanda, Security Council resolution 955 (1994), annex, Art. 2.

the elements of the crime, such as the unlawfulness of the act and the *mens rea*.[4] There is also widespread legislative practice recognizing the non-derogability of the prohibition of genocide.[5] The view that the prohibition of genocide is a norm of *jus cogens* has also been expressed by States before organs of the United Nations.[6]

The conclusion of the Commission that the prohibition of aggression has the status of *jus cogens* is strongly supported by State practice in the form of resolutions of the United Nations. General Assembly resolution 3314 (XXIX), on the definition of aggression, provides evidence of the acceptance and recognition of the prohibition against aggression as *jus cogens*.[7] The resolution, adopted by consensus, defines aggression as 'the most serious and dangerous form of the illegal use of force' and 'the possible threat of a world conflict and all its catastrophic consequences'.[8] Moreover, the preamble makes plain 'that territory of a State shall not be violated by being the object, even temporarily, of military occupation or of other measures of force taken by another State in contravention of the Charter'.[9] The prohibition, moreover, is not subject to any derogation.[10] Other evidence cited by the Special Rapporteur consists of 'uncontradicted statements by Governments in the course of the 1966 Vienna Conference', including several pronouncements that explicitly identified the prohibition of aggression

---

[4] For example, mental illness (Art. 31, para. 1(a), of the Rome Statute) excludes the fault element, while self-defence (Art. 31, para. 1(c), of the Rome Statute) excludes the unlawfulness of any conduct.

[5] See, e.g. Criminal Code of Burkina Faso, Art. 313; Penal Code of Côte d'Ivoire, Art. 317; Criminal Code Amendment Act of 1993 of Ghana, sect. 1; Organization of Prosecutions for Offences constituting the Crime of Genocide or Crimes against Humanity committed since 1 October 1990 of Rwanda, Art. 2; Implementation of the Rome Statute of the International Criminal Court Act of South Africa, Schedule 1, Part 1; United States Code, sect. 50A, § 1091; Law No. 2.889 of 1956 of Brazil, Art. 1; Penal Code of Mexico, sect. 149 *bis*; Penal Code of Nicaragua, Arts 549 and 550; Penal Code of Cuba, Art. 116; Law No. 5710–1950 on the Prevention and Punishment of Genocide of Israel; Penal Code of the Fiji Islands, ch. VIII; Criminal Code of the Republic of Tajikistan Art., 398; Criminal Code of the Republic of Albania, Art. 73; Criminal Code of Austria, Art. 321; Law Concerning the Repression of Grave Violations of International Law of Belgium, Art. 1; Criminal Code of the Czech Republic, Art. 259; Criminal Code of France, Arts 211–212; Penal Code of Finland, sect. 6; Criminal Code of Germany, Art. 220; Genocide Convention Act of Ireland, sect. 2; Law No. 962 of 1967; Penal Code of Portugal, art. 239; Penal Code of Spain, Art. 607; Federal Criminal Code of the Russian Federation, Art. 357.

[6] See, e.g. Belarus (A/C.6/73/SR.26); Mozambique (A/C.6/73/SR.28); Spain (A/C.6/73/SR.29). See also Azerbaijan in the Security Council, 17 October 2012 (S/PV.6849).

[7] General Assembly Resolution 3314 (XXIX) of 14 December 1974, annex, preamble.

[8] Ibid.

[9] Ibid.

[10] Para. 4 of the commentary to Art. 40 of the articles on State responsibility, *Yearbook ... 2001*, vol. II (Part II) and corrigendum, paras 76–77, at p. 112.

as one of several examples of *jus cogens*.[11] Even prior to the adoption of
the 1966 draft articles on the law of treaties, States frequently identified, including in the Security Council,[12] the prohibition of aggression as an example of a norm with the status of *jus cogens*.[13]

There is also widespread treaty practice on the prohibition of torture as a
non-derogable obligation. The Convention against Torture, which has 165
States Parties, prohibits torture and obliges States Parties to take measures
to prevent torture.[14] Article 2 of the Convention against Torture provides
that '[n]o exceptional circumstances whatsoever, whether a state of war
or a threat of war, internal political instability or any other public emergency, may be invoked as a justification of torture', emphasizing the non-
derogability of the prohibition.[15] Similarly Article 7 of the International
Covenant on Civil and Political Rights (ICCPR) prohibits torture and
cruel, inhuman or degrading treatment or punishment. More importantly,
Article 7 is included as a non-derogable right under the Covenant.[16] The
right to be free from torture is also included in the Universal Declaration of
Human Rights[17] and the prohibition is contained in regional human rights
treaties.[18]

---

[11] See Ghana, Official Records of the United Nations Conference on the Law of Treaties,
1st Sess., 53rd meeting, 6 May 1968, para. 15; Uruguay, ibid., para. 48; Cyprus ibid., para. 70;
Soviet Union, ibid., 52nd meeting, 4 May 1968, para. 3; and Kenya, ibid., para. 31.

[12] Japan (S/PV.2350) ('The principle of the non-use of force is, in other words, a peremptory norm of international law.'); Portugal (S/PV.2476) ('No argument relating to the security
of States can be invoked as a pretext for the use of force in conditions which jeopardize the
recognized principles of *jus cogens* and accepted norms of the international community');
Cyprus (S/PV.2537) ('it is guilty of against the Republic of Cyprus by virtue of the use of its
armed forces within the territory of the Republic in contravention of the peremptory norms
of international law'); Azerbaijan (S/PV.6897) ('in particular its peremptory norms such those
prohibiting the threat or use of force'); Peru (S/PV.8262) ('We cannot maintain international
peace and security without respect for the rule of law. For example, one of the cornerstones
of the international order is the prohibition of the use of force in any way that is incompatible
with the Charter of the United Nations.'); and Greece (S/PV.8262) ('the peremptory rule of
the Charter that prohibits the use or the threat of use of force and acts of aggression in international relations is of utmost importance').

[13] See, e.g. Netherlands (A/C.6/SR.781, para. 2); Cyprus (A/C.6/SR.783, para. 18); Brazil
(A/C.6/SR.793, para. 14); and the Federal Republic of Germany (A/C.6/41/SR.14, para. 33).

[14] Convention against Torture, Arts 1 and 2, para. 1, and Arts 4 and 5.

[15] Ibid., Art. 2, para. 2.

[16] ICCPR (New York, 16 December 1966), United Nations, *Treaty Series*, vol. 999, No.
14668, p. 171, at Art. 4, para. 2 ('No derogation from articles 6, 7, 8 (paras 1 and 2), 11, 15, 16
and 18 may be made under this provision').

[17] Universal Declaration of Human Rights (1948), Art. 5 ('No one shall be subjected to torture or to cruel, inhuman or degrading treatment or punishment').

[18] See, e.g. African Charter on Human and Peoples' Rights, Art. 5 ('Every individual shall
have the right to the respect of the dignity inherent in a human being and to the recognition
of his legal status. All forms of exploitation and degradation of man particularly slavery, slave
trade, torture, cruel, inhuman or degrading punishment and treatment shall be prohibited');

As mentioned earlier, the Commission, in its draft articles on crimes against humanity provisionally adopted on first reading in 2017, recognized in the preamble that the prohibition of crimes against humanity is a peremptory norm of general international law.[19] The written responses of States to the preambular paragraph of those draft articles also point to the general recognition of States of the peremptory character of the prohibition of crimes against humanity. Most of the comments did not even mention the inclusion of the paragraph describing the prohibition of crimes against humanity as a peremptory norm of international law—a suggestion that it is such an obvious statement of fact that it does not require mention.[20] Those States that did comment on it, other than France,[21] did so with approval. Belgium, for example noted that that, in the 'draft preamble, it is rightly stated that the prohibition of crimes against humanity is a peremptory norm of general international law (*jus cogens*)'.[22] The written observations of Sierra Leone, similarly, take note of the *jus cogens* status of the prohibition of crimes against humanity when commenting on amnesties.[23]

Evidence of the *jus cogens* status of the prohibition of slavery can be seen in the multilateral treaties and other instruments States have adopted. Slavery was first condemned in an international instrument in the 1815 Declaration Relative to the Universal Abolition of the Slave Trade.[24] In 1948, the Universal Declaration of Human Rights provided that '[n]o one

---

American Convention on Human Rights (San José, 22 November 1969), United Nations, *Treaty Series*, vol. 1144, No. 17955, p. 123, Art. 5, para. 2 ('No one shall be subjected to torture or to cruel, inhuman, or degrading punishment or treatment'); European Convention on Human Rights, Art. 3 ('No one shall be subjected to torture or to inhuman or degrading treatment or punishment'). See especially Art. 15, para. 2, which prohibits derogations from Art. 3.

[19] Para. 4 of the commentary to the preamble, draft articles on crimes against humanity, A/72/10, paras 45–46, at p. 23.
[20] Costa Rica, Cuba, Czech Republic, El Salvador, Estonia, France, Germany, Greece, Israel, Japan, Liechtenstein, Malta, Morocco, New Zealand, Nordic countries (Denmark, Iceland, Sweden, Finland, Norway), Panama, Peru, Portugal, Sierra Leone, Singapore, Switzerland, Ukraine, United Kingdom, and Uruguay. See A/CN.4/726.
[21] Ibid. ('There is some doubt, however, as to the desirability of qualifying the prohibition of crimes against humanity as a peremptory norm of general international law, since the Commission is currently working on the topic "Peremptory norms of general international law (*jus cogens*)", and since the preamble of the Rome Statute of the International Criminal Court itself does not refer to them.').
[22] Ibid. See also the written observations of Panama.
[23] Ibid.
[24] Declaration Relative to the Universal Abolition of the Slave Trade (8 February 1815), *Consolidated Treaty Series*, vol. 63, No. 473. See D. Weissbrodt and Anti-Slavery International, *Abolishing Slavery and its Contemporary Forms* (New York and Geneva, United Nations, 2002; HR/PUB/02/4), p. 3.

shall be held in slavery or servitude' and that 'slavery and the slave trade shall be prohibited in all their forms' (Art. 4). In the Durban Declaration, world leaders acknowledged that 'slavery and the slave trade ... were appalling tragedies in the history of humanity' in part 'because of their abhorrent barbarism'.[25] The Declaration further acknowledged 'that slavery and the slave trade are a crime against humanity and should always have been so'.[26]

The absolute and non-derogable nature of the prohibition on slavery is also evident in modern treaty practice. In the 1926 Slavery Convention, States undertook to prevent and suppress 'slavery' and the 'slave trade'.[27] This obligation was subject to a number of qualifiers, however, raising doubts about the non-derogability of the prohibition at that time.[28] Notably, the obligation to end slavery was progressive, rather than immediate and without limitations and 'as soon as possible'.[29] However, the obligation to impose severe penalties was immediate and not subject to the qualification of progressive eradication. The Convention also allowed the legal continuation of 'forced labour' under certain strict conditions for a transitional period. At the time, slavery was defined as the condition over which some form of ownership was exercised over a person, while forced labour was always compensated and labourers could not be compelled to relocate. The Supplementary Convention of 1956 extended the scope of the prohibition to cover practices similar to slavery, which would include the practice of forced labour.[30]

In addition to the 1926 and 1956 Slavery Conventions, other non-slavery-specific treaties prohibit slavery in absolute and non-derogable terms. The International Covenant on Civil and Political Rights is a clear example. In Article 8, 'slavery and the slave-trade in all their forms' and 'servitude' are prohibited. Moreover, the prohibition of 'slavery and slave-trade

---

[25] Durban Declaration adopted by the World Conference against Racism, Racial Discrimination, Xenophobia and Related Intolerance, contained in *Report of the World Conference against Racism, Racial Discrimination, Xenophobia and Related Intolerance, Durban*, 31 August–8 September 2001, A/CONF.189/12, p. 5, at para. 13.

[26] Ibid.

[27] Slavery Convention (Geneva, 25 September 1926), League of Nations, *Treaty Series*, vol. LX, No. 1414, p. 253, Art. 2(a) and (b).

[28] See J.E. Christófolo, 2016, *Solving Antinomies between Peremptory Norms in Public International Law* (Geneva, Schulthess), p. 216 ('But the 1926 Convention did not peremptorily abolish ... slavery. Article 2 only stipulates that States Parties agreed to upon the obligation to progressively bring about the complete elimination of slavery in all its forms').

[29] Slavery Convention, Art. 2(b).

[30] Supplementary Convention on the Abolition of Slavery, the Slave Trade, and Institutions and Practices Similar to Slavery (Geneva, 7 September 1956), United Nations, *Treaty Series*, vol. 226, No. 3822, p. 40.

in all their forms' and 'servitude' are explicitly excluded from the possibility of derogation.[31] Protocol II to the 1949 Geneva Conventions similarly states that 'slavery and the slave trade in all their forms' 'remain prohibited at any time and in any place whatsoever'.[32] Examples of other treaties that prohibit and/or criminalize slavery in absolute terms include the African Charter on Human and Peoples' Rights,[33] the Rome Statute of the International Criminal Court, which criminalizes slavery as a crime against humanity,[34] and the Protocol to Prevent and Punish Trafficking in Persons.[35]

The complete and total rejection of the policy of apartheid and the discriminatory policies attendant to it, as a crime against humanity and the conscience of mankind, was codified in the International Convention on the Suppression and Punishment of the Crime of Apartheid.[36] In its preamble, the Convention condemned 'racial segregation and apartheid' and committed parties 'to prevent, prohibit and eradicate *all practices*' of racial segregation and apartheid. The Convention declares apartheid to be 'a crime against humanity' and that 'inhuman acts' connected with the crime of apartheid, such as racial segregation and racial discrimination, 'are crimes violating the principles of international law, in particular the purposes and principles of the Charter of the United Nations'. Furthermore, consistent

---

[31] ICCPR, Art. 4, para. 2.

[32] Protocol Additional to the Geneva Conventions of 12 August 1949, and relating to the protection of victims of non-international armed conflicts (Protocol II) (Geneva, 8 June 1977), United Nations, *Treaty Series*, vol. 1125, No. 17513, p. 609, Art. 4, para. 2(f).

[33] African Charter on Human and Peoples' Rights, Art. 5 ('All forms of exploitation and degradation of man particularly slavery, slave trade, torture, cruel, inhuman or degrading punishment and treatment shall be prohibited').

[34] Rome Statute, Art. 7, paras 1(c), and 7, para. 2(c).

[35] Protocol to Prevent, Suppress and Punish Trafficking in Persons, Especially Women and Children, Supplementing the United Nations Convention against Transnational Organized Crime (New York, 15 November 2000), United Nations, *Treaty Series*, vol. 2237, No. 39574, p. 319. See especially definition of 'trafficking' and 'exploitation' in Art. 3(a). See also Art. 3(b), which excludes 'consent' as a justification.

[36] International Convention on the Suppression and Punishment of the Crime of Apartheid (New York, 30 November 1973), United Nations, *Treaty Series*, vol. 1015, No. 14861, p. 243, Art. II. The acts specified in Art. II include: denial to a member or members of a racial group or groups of the right to life and liberty of person by specified means; deliberate imposition on a racial group or groups of living conditions calculated to cause its or their physical destruction in whole or in part; any legislative measures and other measures calculated to prevent a racial group or groups from participation in the political, social, economic, and cultural life of the country; any measures including legislative measures, designed to divide the population along racial lines by the creation of separate reserves and ghettos for the members of a racial group or groups; exploitation of the labour of the members of a racial group or groups; and persecution of organizations and persons, by depriving them of fundamental rights and freedoms, because they oppose apartheid. General Assembly resolution 1514 (XV) on the declaration on the granting of independence to colonial countries and peoples of 14 December 1960, para. 1.

with the consequences of the serious breaches of *jus cogens*, the Convention provides for responsibility 'irrespective of the motive' for anyone who commits or assists or cooperates in the commission of the crime of apartheid.

There is ample other State practice recognizing the prohibition of apartheid and racial discrimination as a peremptory norm of general international law. In 1960, the General Assembly determined that the 'subjection of peoples to alien subjugation, domination and exploitation constitutes a denial of fundamental human rights and is contrary to the Charter of the United Nations'.[37] This declaration laid the foundation for further declarations expressing rejection of the policy of apartheid and racial discrimination. In 1965, for example, the General Assembly declared that '*all* States shall contribute to the complete elimination of racial discrimination and colonialism in all its manifestations'.[38] It is noteworthy that the resolution places an obligation on *all* States, and not only the affected States, to contribute to the eradication of racial discrimination and the domination of people. This, it will be recalled from the third report, is one of the key consequences of peremptory norms of international law—the obligation on all States to cooperate in the elimination of the legal consequences of breaches of *jus cogens*.

What is more, the relevant resolutions not only require States to cooperate in the eradication of the discriminatory policies, but they also *seem to* exempt liberation movements fighting the scourge of apartheid and racial discrimination from particular rules of international law in efforts to liberate peoples from the racial domination and apartheid. For example, the General Assembly resolution on the definition of aggression was subject to the caveat that the definition did not prejudice 'in any way' the right of 'peoples under colonial and racist regimes or other forms of alien domination ... [to] struggle' for their rights and 'to seek and receive support'.[39]

The General Assembly has also adopted South Africa and apartheid-specific resolutions and declarations. In 1975, the General Assembly

---

[37] General Assembly resolution 1514 (XV) of 14 December 1960 on the Declaration on the Granting of Independence to Colonial Countries and Peoples.

[38] General Assembly resolution 2131 (XX) of 21 December 1965 on the Declaration on the Inadmissibility of Intervention in the Domestic Affairs of States and the Protection of their Independence and Sovereignty, para. 6. See also General Assembly resolution 2625 (XXV) on the Declaration of Principles of International Law concerning Friendly Relations and Cooperation among States in accordance with the Charter of the United Nations, annex, para. 1 ('Solemnly proclaim [that] ... States shall cooperate in the promotion of universal respect for, and observance of, human rights and fundamental freedoms for all and in the elimination of all forms of racial discrimination').

[39] General Assembly Resolution on the Definition of Aggression (n 7.)

adopted the resolution on the special responsibility of the United Nations towards the oppressed people of South Africa, in which it proclaimed that 'the United Nations and the international community' owe a duty to the 'oppressed people of South Africa and their liberation movements' to contribute to the end of *apartheid*.[40] Resolution 32/105 J, having reaffirmed 'the legitimacy of the struggle of the oppressed people of South Africa', described the policy of South Africa as 'the criminal policy of *apartheid*'.[41] The resolution went as far as to endorse the 'right to ... struggle for the seizure of power by all available and appropriate means ..., including armed struggle'.[42] Importantly, consistent with the duty to cooperate to bring to an end violations of *jus cogens*, the resolution declared that 'the international community should provide all assistance to the national liberation movement of South Africa' in its struggle to overthrow apartheid.[43] The General Assembly adopted many similar resolutions over a prolonged period of time, describing apartheid as, for example, 'inhuman' and calling on the international community to assist in its eradication.[44] While these resolutions did not use the language of '*jus cogens*' or 'peremptory norms', they did use terms akin to those used to describe genocide and torture.

It is important to recall that it was not just the General Assembly that adopted multiple resolutions on the illegality and inhumanity of apartheid and racial discrimination. The Security Council also adopted its own resolutions. In 1984 the Security Council described apartheid and racial discrimination as 'a crime against the conscience and dignity of mankind' and as being 'incompatible with the rights and dignity of man'[45] similar to the language used by the International Court of Justice in the advisory opinion

---

[40] General Assembly resolution 32/105 J on assistance to the national liberation movement of South Africa of 14 December 1977, paras 2–3.

[41] Ibid., para. 3.

[42] Ibid., para. 3.

[43] Ibid., para. 4.

[44] In addition to those cited above, see General Assembly resolution 31/6 A on the so-called independent Transkei and other bantustans of 26 October 1976, para. 1 ('strongly condemns the establishment of bantustans as designed to consolidate the inhuman policies of *apartheid*'). See also General Assembly resolution 34/93 O of 12 December 1979 on the Declaration on South Africa; General Assembly resolution 39/72 A of 13 December 1984 on comprehensive sanctions against the apartheid regime and support to the liberation struggle in South Africa; and General Assembly resolution 39/72 G of 13 December 1984 on concerted international action for the elimination of *apartheid*. General Assembly resolution 3411 C (XXX) of 28 November 1975 on the special responsibility of the United Nations and the international community towards the oppressed people of South Africa, para. 1.

[45] Security Council resolution 473 (1980), para. 3. See also Security Council resolution 418 (1977); Security Council resolution 554 (1984) and resolution 569 (1985)

on *Reservations to the Convention on Genocide*.[46] Reflecting the duty to co-operate to bring to an end serious breaches of *jus cogens* and not to provide assistance for the maintenance of situations created by such breaches of *jus cogens*, in this case apartheid and racial discrimination, the Security Council provided for members of the United Nations to adopt various sanctions against South Africa.[47]

The right to self-determination is another norm previously identified by the Commission as a norm of *jus cogens*. Its peremptory status is accepted almost universally, except by one State, Israel. In the Sixth Committee debate on the work of the Commission during its seventieth session (2018), the government of Israel expressed the view that, contrary to the Commission's previous conclusions, the *jus cogens* status of self-determination was 'questionable'.[48]

The right to self-determination has been reflected in treaty practice. The Charter of the United Nations, Article 1, provides that the purposes of the United Nations are, inter alia, to 'develop friendly relations among nations based on respect for the cultural development, and every State has the duty to respect this right in accordance with the provisions of the Charter'; 'Every State has the duty to promote, through joint and separate action, realization of the principle of equal rights and self-determination of peoples, in accordance with the provisions of the Charter, and to render assistance to the United Nations in carrying out the responsibilities entrusted to it by the Charter regarding the implementation of the principle'; and 'Every State has the duty to refrain from any forcible action which deprives peoples referred to above in the elaboration of the present principle of their right to self-determination and freedom and independence'.

The *jus cogens* status of the right to self-determination has been recognized in the practice of States in the context of multilateral instruments. There have been many General Assembly resolutions proclaiming the fundamental character of the right to self-determination. Perhaps one of the most important instruments in this respect is the 1960 Declaration on the Granting of Independence to Colonial Countries and Peoples, which

---

[46] *Reservations to the Convention on Genocide*, Advisory Opinion, ICJ Reports 1951, p. 23 ('it was the intention of the United Nations to condemn and punish genocide as "a crime under international law" involving a denial of the right of existence of entire human groups, a denial which shocks the conscience of mankind and results in great losses to humanity, and which is contrary to moral law and to the spirit and aims of the United Nations').

[47] See, e.g. Security Council resolution 418 (1977); Security Council resolution 569 (1985); and Security Council resolution 591 (1986).

[48] Israel (A/C.6/73/SR.27).

provided for a right to self-determination in absolute terms and was referred to by the International Court of Justice in establishing the *erga omnes* nature of the right.[49] Equally important is the 1970 Declaration on Principles of International Law concerning Friendly Relations and Cooperation among States in accordance with the Charter of the United Nations.[50] In the preamble to that declaration, the principle of self-determination is described as 'significant'.[51] In several places the declaration stresses the importance of the right to self-determination.[52] The 1965 Declaration on the Inadmissibility of Intervention in the Domestic Affairs of States and the Protection of their Independence and Sovereignty, for its part, provided that '[a]ll States shall respect the right of self-determination and independence of peoples and nations, to be freely exercised without any foreign pressure, and with absolute respect for human rights and fundamental freedoms'.[53] The importance and fundamental character of the right to self-determination are evident from the fact that General Assembly resolution 3314 (XXIX) on the definition of aggression provided that none of the rules identified by the Assembly on aggression 'could in any way prejudice the right to self-determination'.[54] The fundamental character of the right to self-determination has also been affirmed in country-specific resolutions. The General Assembly has

---

[49] General Assembly resolution 1514 (XV), especially paras 1 and 2. See *Legal Consequences for States of the Continued Presence of South Africa in Namibia (South West Africa) notwithstanding, Security Council Resolution 276 (1970)*, Advisory Opinion, ICJ Reports 1971, p. 31, para. 52, where the Court considered the Declaration as a 'further important stage' in the development of the *erga omnes* applicability of the right of self-determination 'which embraces all peoples and territories which "have not yet attained independence"'.

[50] General Assembly resolution 2625 (XXV) of 24 October 1970, annex.

[51] Ibid., 14th preambular para.

[52] For example: 'By virtue of the principle of equal rights and self-determination of peoples enshrined in the Charter of the United Nations, all peoples have the right freely to determine, without external interference, their political status and to pursue their economic, social and cultural development, and every State has the duty to respect this right in accordance with the provisions of the Charter.'

[53] General Assembly resolution 3314 (XXIX), annex, Art. 7. General Assembly res. 2131 (XX), annex, para. 6.

[54] See, e.g. General Assembly resolution 66/146 of 19 December 2011 on the right of the Palestinian people to self-determination, which, in its preamble, recalls the International Court of Justice's description of the right to self-determination as establishing an *erga omnes* obligation and, in para. 1, reaffirms the right of Palestine to self-determination. See also General Assembly resolution 67/19 of 29 November 2012 on the status of Palestine in the United Nations, which, for example, refers to 'the inalienable rights of the Palestinian people, primarily the right to self-determination' (9th preambular para.). On South Africa, see, for example, General Assembly resolution 32/105 J, para. 2, and resolution 34/93 O, para. 3.

also declared an agreement invalid on account of it being inconsistent with the right to self-determination.[55]

The Security Council has itself also affirmed the right to self-determination, albeit not as often or as directly as the General Assembly.[56] In resolution 384 (1975), the Council recognized 'the inalienable right of the people of Timor-Leste to self-determination' and called upon all States to respect that right.[57] The resolution also applied the consequences of serious breaches of *jus cogens*, namely the duty to cooperate to bring to an end situations created by the breach, to the breach of the right of self-determination of the people of Timor-Leste.[58]

Both the International Covenant on Civil and Political Rights and the International Covenant on Economic, Social and Cultural Rights proclaim that '[a]ll peoples have the right of self-determination. By virtue of that right they freely determine their political status and freely pursue their economic, social and cultural development'.[59] In its general comment No. 12, the Human Rights Committee observed that the 'right of self-determination is of particular importance because its realization is an essential condition for the effective' protection of human rights.[60] According to the Committee, that was the reason that States included the right 'in a provision of positive law in both Covenants and placed this provision as Article 1 apart from and before all of the other rights in the two Covenants'.[61] The Committee described it as an 'inalienable right'. Importantly, according to the Committee,

---

[55] General Assembly resolution 33/28 A of 7 December 1978 on the question of Palestine, para. 4 ('the validity of agreements purporting to solve the problem of Palestine requires that they be within the framework of the United Nations and its Charter and its resolutions on the basis of the full attainment and exercise of the inalienable rights of the Palestinian people, including the right of return and the right to national independence and sovereignty in Palestine, and with the participation of the Palestine Liberation Organization').

[56] See, for an example of an indirect affirmation of the right to self-determination, Security Council resolution 554 (1984), preamble ('Reaffirming the legitimacy of the struggle of the oppressed people of South Africa for the elimination of *apartheid* and for the establishment of a society in which all the people of South Africa as a whole, irrespective of race, colour, sex or creed, will enjoy equal and full political and other rights and participate freely in the determination of their destiny').

[57] Security Council resolution 384 (1975), preamble and para. 1.

[58] Ibid., para. 4 ('Urges all States and other parties to cooperate fully with the efforts of the United Nations to achieve a peaceful solution to the existing situation and to facilitate the decolonisation of the Territory'). See also Security Council resolution 389 (1976).

[59] International Covenant on Civil and Political Rights; International Covenant on Economic, Social and Cultural Rights, common Art. 1 (New York, 16 December 1966), *UN Treaty Series* 993, No. 14531, p. 3.

[60] Human Rights Committee, General Comment No. 12 (1984) GAOR 39th Sess., Supp. No. 40 (A/39/40), annex VI, para. 1.

[61] Ibid.

the obligations flowing from the right exist independent of the Covenants.[62] The African Charter on Human and Peoples' Rights provides that '[a]ll peoples shall have the right to existence' and that they 'shall have the unquestionable and inalienable right to self-determination'.[63]

5.2 International Jurisprudence

National and international tribunals have begun to address some of the possible consequences deriving from the identification of *jus cogens* norms, such as the impact of peremptory norms on State and official immunities and the immunity of international organizations, as well as in judging the legality of Security Council resolutions and incompatible domestic laws. Various studies of the ILC, in particular the commentary to Article 26 of the articles on State responsibility[64] as well as Section E of the Report of the Study Group on Fragmentation, also provide some insights.[65] Nonetheless, in the absence of more jurisprudence and state practice, the effects and consequences of *jus cogens* remain largely theoretical. Moreover, while significant evidence of international law, the jurisprudence of international courts and tribunals is only an indirect source of State practice.

As indicated above, the list in the Commission's commentaries to the articles on State responsibility represents the most widely cited examples of *jus cogens*. This, in the view of the Special Rapporteur, is the *only* objective means by which to determine which norms to include and which norms to exclude in a potential illustrative list as part of a draft conclusion. The Rapporteur notes that *any* list, 'even if as accurate and comprehensive as possible' is likely to be questioned and unsatisfactory to some.[66] In particular, 'it is likely to be criticized for not including other deserving norms'. He responded with two points: first, the list in the draft conclusion simply confirms a previous list of *jus cogens* norms identified by the Commission.

---

[62] Ibid., paras 2 and 6 ('The obligations exist irrespective of whether a people entitled to self-determination depends on a State party to the Covenant or not. It follows that all States parties to the Covenant should take positive action to facilitate realization of and respect for the right of peoples to self-determination').

[63] African Charter on Human and Peoples' Rights, Art. 20, para. 1.

[64] International Law Commission, draft articles on the responsibility of States for internationally wrongful acts, with commentaries, 53rd sess. of the ILC, UN Doc. A/56/10, 2001, at 84–85.

[65] Fragmentation of international law, paras 329–409.

[66] See, for a critique, H. Charlesworth and C. Chinkin, 1993, 'The gender of *jus cogens*', 15 *Human Rights Q.*, 63–76.

Other norms of *jus cogens* can exist and the draft conclusion makes it clear that its list is not exhaustive. Second, to the extent that any norm has not acquired the status of *jus cogens* because of insufficient recognition and acceptance by the international community of States as a whole, nothing prevents it from acquiring the status of *jus cogens* in the future. Indeed, the work of the Commission may serve to generate further evidence of acceptance and recognition by the international community of States as a whole for additional norms to be added to the list.

a. Jurisprudence of international courts and tribunals

The International Court of Justice's judgment in the *Corfu Channel* case may reflect the notion of obligatory general principles described in this section. Although the Court did not expressly refer to *jus cogens*, it held that Albania's obligations were founded in certain general and well-recognized principles, namely: 'elementary considerations of humanity, even more exacting in peace than in war, the principle of the freedom of maritime communication; and every State's obligation not to allow knowingly its territory to be used for acts contrary to the rights of other States'.[67] Although not mentioning peremptory norms or *jus cogens*, the suggestion is implicit that these elementary considerations of humanity that are more exacting in peacetime than during wartime may indeed be non-derogable and thus peremptory.

Turning to specific norms on the Rapporteur's list, the most widely cited example of the recognition of the *prohibition of aggression* as a norm *jus cogens* is the *Military and Paramilitary Activities* case, although the Court in its judgment never expressly affirms the assertion, instead citing the Commission's own view on the issue.[68] Many texts have been written about whether the Court's comment can be seen as support for the prohibition of aggression as a norm *jus cogens*.[69] The Court refers only to the 'statements by State representatives' and the Commission 'in the course of its work on the codification of the law of treaties' rather than including an express

---

[67] *Corfu Channel Case (United Kingdom of Great Britain and Northern Ireland v Albania)*, ICJ, Merits, Judgment of 9 April 1949, at 22.

[68] *Military and Paramilitary Activities in and against Nicaragua (Nicaragua. v United States)* Merits, Judgment, ICJ Reports 1986, p. 14, at p. 100, para. 190.

[69] First report (A/CN.4/693), para. 46.

affirmation of its own. Notably, the Commission itself, in its commentary to Article 40 of the articles on State responsibility, took the view that the Court had recognized the *jus cogens* status of the prohibition of aggression.[70]

The ambivalence of the International Court in the *Military and Paramilitary Activities* case, may have been resolved, however, in the *Kosovo* advisory opinion, wherein the Court stated that the illegality attached to previous declarations in the matter 'stemmed, not from the unilateral character of the declarations as such, but from the fact that they were, or would have been, connected with the unlawful use of force or other egregious violations of norms of general international law, in particular those of a peremptory character'.[71]

As for the *prohibition of torture*, the International Court of Justice, in the *Belgium v Senegal* case, explicitly recognized that the prohibition of torture is not only 'part of customary international law ... [but] it has become a peremptory norm (*jus cogens*)'[72] This followed the International Criminal Tribunal for the former Yugoslavia (ICTY) Trial Chamber judgment in 1998 in *Prosecutor v Delalić* that had already made the same determination.[73] A month later, in *Prosecutor v Furundžija*, the Tribunal's Trial Chamber confirmed that 'because of ... the values it protects', the prohibition of torture 'has evolved into a peremptory norm or *jus cogens*'.[74] Those Trial Chamber judgments were affirmed by the Appeals Chamber of the Tribunal.[75]

---

[70] Para. (4) of the commentary to Art. 40 of the articles on State responsibility, *Yearbook ... 2001*, vol. II (Part II) and corrigendum, paras 76–77, at p. 112, referring to 'the submissions of both parties in the *Military and Paramilitary Activities in and against Nicaragua* case and the Court's own position in that case' as evidence of the peremptory status of the prohibition of aggression.

[71] *Accordance with International Law of the Unilateral Declaration of Independence in Respect of Kosovo*, Advisory Opinion, ICJ Reports 2010, p. 403, at p. 437, para. 81.

[72] *Questions relating to the Obligation to Prosecute or Extradite (Belgium v Senegal) Judgment*, ICJ Reports 2012, p. 422, at 457, para. 99.

[73] *Prosecutor v Zejnil Delalić, Zdravko Mucić also known as 'Pavo', Hazim Delić, Esad Landžo also known as 'Zenga'*, No. IT-96-21-T, Judgment, Trial Chamber, ICTY, 16 November 1998, *Judicial Reports 1998*, para. 454 ('Based on the foregoing, it can be said that the prohibition of torture is a norm of customary international law. It further constitutes a norm of *jus cogens*.'). See also *Prosecutor v Dragoljub Kunarac* et al., No. IT-96-23-T, Judgment, Trial Chamber, ICTY, 22 February 2001, para. 466, among several other judgments of the Tribunal recognizing the prohibition of torture as *jus cogens*.

[74] *Prosecutor v Anto Furundžija*, No. IT-95-17/1, Judgment, ICTY, 10 December 1998, Judicial Reports 1998, paras 153–156.

[75] *Prosecutor v Zejnil Delalić, Zdravko Mucić (aka 'Pavo'), Hazim Deli and Esad Landžo (aka 'Zenga')*, No. IT-96-21-A, Judgment, Appeals Chamber, ICTY, 20 February 2001, para. 172, in particular footnote 225.

As with the prohibition of torture, the ICJ has expressly recognized the *prohibition of genocide* as a norm *jus cogens*. In the *Reservations to the Convention on Genocide* advisory opinion, the Court does not use the terms '*jus cogens*', 'peremptory norms', or even '*erga omnes* obligations', but the language the Court uses to describes the prohibition of genocide is consistent with the description of *jus cogens*.[76] In the advisory opinion, the Court made the following remarks:

> The origins of the Convention show that it was the intention of the United Nations to condemn and punish genocide as 'a crime under international law' involving a denial of the right of existence of entire human groups, a denial which shocks the conscience of mankind and results in great losses to humanity, and which is contrary to moral law and to the spirit and aims of the United Nations (Resolution 96 (I) of the General Assembly, December 11th 1946). The first consequence arising from this conception is that the principles underlying the Convention are principles which are recognized by civilized nations as binding on States, even without any conventional obligation. A second consequence is the universal character both of the condemnation of genocide and of the co-operation required 'in order to liberate mankind from such an odious scourge' (Preamble to the Convention). The Genocide Convention was therefore intended by the General Assembly and by the contracting parties to be definitely universal in scope.[77]

Although the Court does not ascribe the status of *jus cogens* to the prohibition of genocide contained in the *Convention on the Prevention and Punishment of the Crime of Genocide*,[78] the language used reflects the general nature of peremptory norms.[79] More than half a century later, the ICJ affirmed the *jus cogens* character of the prohibition of genocide, repeating the quote from the 1951 advisory opinion[80] before stating that 'it follows that' the prohibition contained in the Genocide Convention constitutes an *erga omnes* obligation and a norm of *jus cogens*.[81] The Court has also

---

[76] *Reservations to the Convention on Genocide* (n 46) at, p. 15.

[77] Ibid., p. 23.

[78] Convention on the Prevention and Punishment of the Crime of Genocide (Paris, 9 December 1948), United Nations, *Treaty Series*, vol. 78, No. 1021, p. 277.

[79] See statement of the Chair of the Drafting Committee of 26 July 2017, annex.

[80] *Armed Activities on the Territory of the Congo (New Application: 2002) (Democratic Republic of the Congo v Rwanda), Jurisdiction and Admissibility*, ICJ Reports 2006, p. 6, at pp. 31–32, para. 64.

[81] Ibid.

confirmed the *jus cogens* character of the prohibition of genocide in subsequent cases[82] and the characterization has been supported in dissenting and separate opinions of the Court.[83] As with the prohibition of torture, the prohibition of genocide had also been recognized as *jus cogens* in the ICTY and the International Criminal Tribunal for Rwanda (ICTR).[84]

The ICJ addressed one of the possible consequences of finding the prohibition of genocide to be a norm *jus cogens* in denying the Democratic of Congo's assertion in its case against Rwanda that Rwanda's reservation to the Genocide Convention was invalid because it violated a peremptory norm.[85] The ICJ held that the reservation was not invalid because no such norm required a State to consent to the Court's jurisdiction in order to settle a dispute relating to the Genocide Convention. Significantly, the Democratic Republic of the Congo (DRC) and Rwanda agreed that the substantive provisions of the Convention have the status of *jus cogens* and create rights and obligations *erga omnes*, but Rwanda argued that this was insufficient to confer jurisdiction.[86] The Court accepted the DRC's argument that a reservation to Article IX of the Genocide Convention was

---

[82] See also *Case Concerning Application of the Convention on the Prevention and Punishment of the Crime of Genocide (Bosnia and Herzegovina v Serbia and Montenegro), ICJ Reports 2007*, p. 43, at pp. 110–111, para. 161, where the Court, having quoted the 1951 advisory opinion, states that it, in the 2006 judgment, had 'reaffirmed the 1951 ... statement[] ... *when* it added that the norm prohibiting genocide was assuredly a peremptory norm of international law (*jus cogens*)'. In the *Armed Activities on the Territory of the Congo* (n 80), pp. 31–32, para. 64 ('the fact that a dispute relates to compliance with a norm having such a character [of *jus cogens*], which is assuredly the case with regard to the prohibition of genocide, cannot of itself provide a basis for the jurisdiction of the Court'); *Application of the Convention on the Prevention and Punishment of the Crime of Genocide (Croatia v Serbia)*, ICJ Reports 2015, p. 3, at pp. 47–48, para. 88.

[83] First among these was the separate opinion of Judge *ad hoc* Lauterpacht in the *Application of the Convention on the Prevention and Punishment of the Crime of Genocide, Provisional Measures*, Order of 13 September 1993, ICJ Reports 1993, p. 325, at p. 440, para. 100 ('the prohibition of genocide has long been regarded as one of the few undoubted examples of *jus cogens*').

[84] See, e.g. *Prosecutor v Zoran Kupreškić et al.*, IT-95-16-T, Judgment, Trial Chamber, ICTY, Judicial Reports 2000, para. 520; *Prosecutor v Radislav Krstić*, IT-98-33-T, Judgment, Trial Chamber, ICTY, 2 August 2001, para. 541; *Prosecutor v Milomir Stakić*, IT-97-24-T, Judgment, Trial Chamber, ICTY, 31 July 2003; *Prosecutor v Vidoje Blagojević and Dragan Jokić*, IT-02-60-T, Judgment, Trial Chamber, ICTY, 17 January 2005. For decisions of the ICTR see, for example, *Prosecutor v Clément Kayishema and Obed Ruzindana*, ICTR-95-1-T, Judgment, ICTR, 21 May 1999, *Reports of Orders, Decisions and Judgements 1999*, vol. II, para. 88 ('The Genocide Convention became widely accepted as an international human rights instrument. Furthermore, the crime of genocide is considered part of international customary law and, moreover, a norm of *jus cogens*.')

[85] Case concerning Armed Activities on the Territory of the Congo (new application) (Jurisdiction of the Court and Admissibility of the Application), 3 February 2006, paras 56–64.

[86] Ibid., para. 60.

compatible with the object and purpose of the Convention, noting that 14 other States Parties have similar reservations and the majority of the 133 other states did not object to them; it also reaffirmed that the rights and obligations are *erga omnes* and, moreover, are norms of a peremptory character, but held that this finding was independent of the requirement of consent to jurisdiction.[87] According to the Court, 'the fact that a dispute relates to compliance with a norm having such a character, *which is assuredly the case with regard to the prohibition of genocide,* cannot of itself provide the basis for the jurisdiction of the Court to entertain that dispute'.[88]

The Court also affirmed this decision in rejecting the DRC's argument the Rwanda's reservation to Convention on the Elimination of All Forms of Racial Discrimination[89] was similarly in violation of a peremptory norm of international law. The Court again insisted that there is no peremptory norm requiring States to consent to its jurisdiction to settle disputes relating to the Racial Convention even if the prohibition of racial discrimination is such a norm. A final argument was also rejected: that Article 66 of the Vienna Convention on the Law of Treaties established the jurisdiction of the Court to settle any dispute arising from the violation of peremptory norms in the area of human rights, as those norms are reflected in a number of international instruments. The Court concluded it lacked jurisdiction over the matter.[90]

A separate opinion of five judges called on the Court to revisit its opinion that reservations to Article IX of the Genocide Convention are compatible with that treaty's object and purpose. Ad hoc judge John Dugard added his own separate opinion in which he elaborated on the role of jus cogens in international litigation and the limits on its use. Judge Dugard agreed with the decision of the Court that it lacked jurisdiction over the dispute and with the decision of the Court that it could not force jurisdiction on a state, even for alleged violations of *jus cogens* norms. As he says in his opinion, 'the approval given to jus cogens by the Court in the present judgment is to be welcomed. However, the judgment stresses that the scope of jus cogens is not unlimited and that the concept is not to be used as an instrument to overthrow accepted doctrines of international law'.[91] Although it may

[87] Ibid., para. 64 citing the *East Timor Case (Portugal v Australi*a) ICJ Reports 1995, p. 102, para. 29.

[88] Ibid. (emphasis added).

[89] New York, 21 December 1965.

[90] Rwanda had asserted violation by the DRC of the UN Charter, numerous human rights treaties, and various other treaties.

[91] Separate Opinion of ad hoc Judge John Dugard, para. 6.

seem that he is leaving no scope for jus cogens in practice, he in fact goes on to explain its role in relation to the hierarchy of norms and judicial choice when faced with conflicting norms and policies. 'The fact that norms of jus cogens advance both principle and policy means that they must inevitably play a dominant role in the process of judicial choice.'[92]

There is little international litigation over what may be termed classical slavery. As a result, the International Court of Justice has not had to rule on the *prohibition of slavery* and has thus not addressed the status of the ban on slavery as a norm of *jus cogens*. As with the prohibition of apartheid and racial discrimination, the Court's recognition of the *jus cogens* status of the prohibition of slavery has been indirect, mostly through its inclusion on the list of rules creating *erga omnes* obligations.[93] Yet, the prohibition of slavery is one of the main examples given of peremptory norms of international law.[94] Its recognition as a norm from which no derogation is permitted can be seen in the practice of States, particularly in the context of multilateral instruments, as discussed in the previous section.

In his fourth report, the Special Rapporteur decided to use the phrase '*the prohibition of apartheid and racial discrimination*' in general. The phrase of is meant to indicate or signify 'a composite act, namely the prohibition of apartheid with racial discrimination as an integral part of that'.[95] In this regard, the International Convention on the Suppression and Punishment of Apartheid defines apartheid in a broad sense to include 'similar policies and practices of racial segregation and discrimination as practiced in southern Africa' and covers and a number of specified acts.[96] Notably, too, acts of

---

[92] Ibid., para. 10. Judge Koroma in his dissent takes the issue further and would have the Court find the reservation to Art. IX of the Genocide Convention to be void as not in conformity with a norm of *jus cogens*.

[93] *Barcelona Traction, Light and Power Company, Limited (Belgium v Spain)*, ICJ, Second Phase, Judgment of 5 February 1970, p. 32, para. 34.

[94] Christófolo (n 28) at p. 216 ('The prohibition of slavery is placed among the first undisputable peremptory norms that emerged in contemporary international law').

[95] Fourth report on peremptory norms of general international law (*jus cogens*) by Dire Tladi, Special Rapporteur, International Law Commission 71st Sess., Geneva, 29 April–7 June and 8 July–9 August 2019 (A/CN.4/727) 31 January 2019, at para. 91.

[96] International Convention on the Suppression and Punishment of the Crime of Apartheid (New York, 30 November 1973), United Nations, *Treaty Series*, vol. 1015, No. 14861, p. 243, Art. II. The acts specified in Art. II include: denial to a member or members of a racial group or groups of the right to life and liberty of person by specified means; deliberate imposition on a racial group or groups of living conditions calculated to cause its or their physical destruction in whole or in part; any legislative measures and other measures calculated to prevent a racial group or groups from participation in the political, social, economic, and cultural life of the country; any measures, including legislative measures, designed to divide the population along racial lines by the creation of separate reserves and ghettos for the members of a racial group or groups; exploitation of the labour of the members of a racial group or groups; and

apartheid are prohibited as crimes against humanity. If crimes against humanity are *jus cogens*, then acts of apartheid, as crimes against humanity, would also constitute violations of *jus cogens*. In the *Namibia* advisory opinion, the Court determined that the apartheid and racial policies of South Africa constituted 'a denial of fundamental human rights [that] is a flagrant violation of the purposes and principles of the Charter'.[97] This is an early indication that the International Court of Justice might now include it as an example of a *jus cogens* norm, but the Court has not explicitly made such a determination. In its famous declaration in the *Barcelona Traction* case, however, the Court included the prohibition of racial discrimination among norms with an *erga omnes* quality. The Court stated that obligations

> *erga omnes* derive, for example, in contemporary international law, from the outlawing of acts of aggression, and of genocide, as also from the principles and rules concerning the basic rights of the human person, including protection from slavery and racial discrimination.[98]

The International Law Commission has recognized *the prohibition of crimes against humanity* as a norm of *jus cogens* in the preamble of the draft articles on crimes against humanity, adopted on first reading during the sixty-ninth session.[99] As the Commission noted in the commentary to the preamble, the International Court of Justice, by recognizing the prohibition of torture as *jus cogens* in *Belgium v Senegal a fortiori* suggests that committing acts of torture on a widespread or systematic basis would constitute a crime against humanity and thus would also violate a norm of *jus cogens*.[100] The peremptory status of the prohibition of crimes against humanity has also been affirmed in judgments of the International Tribunal for the Former Yugoslavia. In *Prosecutor v Kupreškić*, the Trial Chamber of the Tribunal held that the prohibition of crimes against humanity along with the prohibition of genocide constituted peremptory norms of general international law.[101]

---

persecution of organizations and persons, by depriving them of fundamental rights and freedoms, because they oppose apartheid.

[97] See *Namibia* (n 49) at, p. 16, at p. 57, para. 131.
[98] *Barcelona Traction* (n 93), at p. 32, para. 34.
[99] Para. (4) of commentary to preamble to the draft articles on crimes against humanity, A/72/10, paras 45–46, at p. 23.
[100] *Belgium v Senegal* (n 72), para. 99.
[101] *Kupreškić* (n 84), para. 520.

The 1863 Lieber Code,[102] generally regarded as the first (national) co-dification of the customary laws of war as applicable at the time, stated that 'all rape' against persons in the invaded country is prohibited.[103] The 1949 Geneva Conventions and 1977 Additional Protocols expressly prohibit rape in certain provisions,[104] as well as misbehaviour that would include sexual violence.[105] Moreover, the fundamental guarantees contained in Article 75 of Additional Protocol I, for any person in the power of a Party to the conflict, include the prohibition of 'outrages upon personal dignity, in particular humiliating and degrading treatment, enforced prostitution and any form of indecent assault'. In addition, various chambers of the ICTY have held that rape or other forms of sexual assault are prohibited under customary international law, thus qualifying as a war crime.[106] With respect to slavery, the Chamber recalls that it is prohibited in all forms under Additional Protocol II,[107] which therefore includes sexual slavery. Sexual slavery can also be considered to fall within the general prohibitions on indecent assault and attacks against honour as applicable to rape,

---

[102] ICC, *Prosecutor v Ntaganda (Bosco)*, Second Decision on the defence's challenge to the jurisdiction of the Court in respect of Counts 6 and 9, Case No. ICC-01/04-02/061707, 4 January 2017, para. 46.

[103] Art. 44 of the Instructions for the Government of Armies of the United States in the Field of 24 April 1863.

[104] See Art. 27 of the Fourth Geneva Convention of 1949; Art. 76 of Additional Protocol I; and Art. 4(2)(e) of Additional Protocol II.

[105] See Art. 12 of the First Geneva Convention of 1949; Art. 12 of the Second Geneva Convention of 1949; Art. 14 of the Third Geneva Convention of 1949; Arts 75 and 77 of Additional Protocol I; and Common Art. 3 (prohibiting 'violence to life and person', including cruel treatment, torture, and 'outrages upon personal dignity').

[106] The ICTY recalled in the Furundžija case that 'rape in time of war is specifically prohibited by treaty law: the Geneva Conventions of 1949, Additional Protocol I of 1977 and Additional Protocol II of 1977. Other serious sexual assaults are expressly or implicitly prohibited in various provisions of the same treaties'. ICTY, *Prosecutor v Furundžija*, Case No. IT-95-17/1, Trial Judgment, 10 December 1998, para. 165. Footnotes omitted. See also ICTY, *Prosecutor v Furundžija*, Case No. IT-95-17/1, Decision on the Defendant's Motion to Dismiss Counts 13 and 14 of the Indictment (Lack of Subject Matter Jurisdiction), 29 May 1998, para. 13 ('[t]he argument that "torture and outrages upon personal dignity including rape are not covered by Article 3 of the Statute" is a misinterpretation of the Statute. Such acts are prohibited under customary international law at all times. […] [I]n times of armed conflict, they also amount to violations of the laws or customs of war, which include the prohibitions in the Hague Conventions of 1907 and Common Article 3'); ICTY, *Prosecutor v Delalić et al.* (Case No. IT-96-21-T, Trial Judgment, 16 November 1998, para. 476). Prior to these judgments, Meron noted that '[r]ape by soldiers has of course been prohibited by the law of war for centuries'. (T. Meron, 1993, 'Rape as a Crime under International Humanitarian Law', 87 *Am. J. Int'l Law* 424–428, at 425.) See also M.C. Bassiouni, 1999, *Crimes against Humanity in International Criminal Law* (2nd rev. edn, The Hague, Martinus Nijhoff), p. 348, who submits that '[r]ape has long been considered a war crime under customary international law'.

[107] Art. 4(2)(f) of Additional Protocol II.

as well as enforced prostitution.[108] Moreover, the prohibitions on rape and (sexual) slavery also form part of customary international humanitarian law, applicable both in times of international and non-international armed conflicts.[109]

While most of the express prohibitions of rape and sexual slavery under international humanitarian law appear in contexts protecting civilians and persons hors de combat in the power of a Party to the conflict, the ICC Chamber in this case did not consider that aspect to exhaustively define or limit the scope of the protection against such conduct.[110] The Chamber in fact, cited the Martens clause,[111] which states that in situations not covered by specific agreements, 'civilians and combatants remain under the protection and authority of the principles of international law derived from established custom, from the principles of humanity and from the dictates of public conscience'.[112] The Chamber additionally notes that the fundamental guarantees provisions refer to acts that 'are and shall remain prohibited at any time and in any place whatsoever' and as such apply to, and protect, all persons in the power of a Party to the conflict.[113]

Indeed, although international humanitarian law allows combatants to participate directly in hostilities and to target combatant members of the opposing forces as well as civilians directly participating in hostilities, there is never a justification to engage in sexual violence against any person;

---

[108] The concept of enforced prostitution as prohibited by Art. 27 of the Fourth Geneva Convention of 1949 did not require a 'pecuniary or other advantage', as is the case for the elements of the war crime of enforced prostitution as included in the Statute, and therefore encompasses conduct that now might be more appropriately charged as sexual slavery (see Jean Pictet et al., 1958, *Commentary to the Fourth Geneva Convention of 1949* (ICRC), p. 205).

[109] As an expression thereof, see Rules 93 and 94 and the underlying practice of the ICRC Study on Customary IHL. See also M. Al-Shible, 2018, 'The role of the advisory opinion of the International Court of Justice in establishing the rules of International Humanitarian Law', 72 *J. Law, Policy and Globalization* 107–110, at 107.

[110] *Ntaganda* case (n 102), para. 47.

[111] The Martens Clause was first included in the preamble to the 1899 Hague Convention on the Laws and Customs of War on Land, and has since been restated in the 1949 Geneva Conventions and 1977 Additional Protocols (see the common article on denunciation in the 1949 Geneva Conventions (i.e. Arts. 63, 62, 142, and 158, respectively); and more specifically Art. 1(2) of Additional Protocol I and the Preamble of Additional Protocol II). See also ICJ, *Legality of the Threat or Use of Nuclear Weapons*, Advisory Opinion, 8 July 1996, paras 78 and 87; ICTY, *Prosecutor v Furundžija*, Case No. IT-95-17/1, Trial Judgment, 10 December 1998, para. 137; and United States Military Tribunal in Nuremberg, Krupp et al., Case No. 214, Judgment of 31 July 1948, Para. 111.

[112] The scope (and working) of the Martens Clause as set out by the International Law Commission, in the United Nations Report of the International Law Commission on the Work of its 46th Sess., 1994, GAOR A/49/10, p. 317.

[113] Art. 75 of Additional Protocol I refers to 'a Party to the conflict' and therefore does not limit the fundamental guarantees to persons in the power of the opposing party.

irrespective of whether or not this person may be liable to be targeted and killed under international humanitarian law.[114]

The Chamber finds additional support for protection against sexual violence under international humanitarian law in the fact that sexual slavery has been recognized as constituting a particular form of slavery.[115] In this regard, the Chamber recalls that the first element of the Elements of Crimes of the war crime of sexual slavery is identical to the Statute's definition of 'enslavement', as set out in Article 7(2)(c),[116] and is based on the definition of slavery as included in the Slavery Convention of 1926.[117] Moreover, just as the prohibition of slavery is a *jus cogens* norm, so today the war crime of sexual slavery has reached that status in international law.[118] As a consequence, the Chamber concludes, 'of the prohibition against rape and sexual slavery being peremptory norms, such conduct is prohibited at all times, both in times of peace and during armed conflicts, and against all persons, irrespective of any legal status'.[119]

The jurisprudence of the ICTY has also, in some instances, identified torture, when committed as a crime against humanity, as a violation of a peremptory norm of general international law. In *Prosecutor v Simić*, the accused had been 'convicted of two counts of torture, as crimes against

[114] Sivakumaran suggests that '[s]exual violence is prohibited, whether against civilians, members of the armed forces, or the armed group'. S. Sivakumaran, 2012, *The Law of Non-International Armed Conflict* (Oxford, Oxford University Press), p. 249.

[115] See, e.g. Pre-Trial Chamber I, *The Prosecutor v Germain Katanga and Mathieu Ngudjolo Chui*, Decision on the confirmation of charges, 30 September 2008. ICC-01/04-01/07-717, paras 430–431; and ICTY, *Prosecutor v Kunarac et al.*, Case No. IT-96-23 and IT-96-23/1-A, Appeals Judgment, 12 June 2002, paras 117–124.

[116] The first element of the war crime of sexual slavery requires that '[t]he perpetrator exercised any or all of the powers attaching to the right of ownership over one or more persons'. Pursuant to Article 7(2)(c) of the Statute, '[e]nslavement' means the exercise of any or all of the powers attaching to the right of ownership over a person.

[117] The Slavery Convention defines slavery in Article 1(1) as 'the status or condition of a person over whom any or all of the powers attaching to the right of ownership are exercised'. See also K. Dörmann, 2002, *Elements of War Crimes under the Rome Statute of the International Criminal Court* (Cambridge, Cambridge University Press), p. 328.

[118] See, the Special Court for Sierra Leone, *Prosecutor v Brima et al.*, SCSL-04-16-T, Judgment, Trial Chamber II, 20 June 2007, para. 705 ('slavery for the purpose of sexual abuse is a jus cogens prohibition in the same manner as slavery for the purpose of physical labour'.); Final report submitted by Special Rapporteur Gay J. McDougall, Contemporary Forms of Slavery—Systematic rape, sexual slavery and slavery like practices during armed conflict, Commission on Human Rights, Sub-Commission on Prevention of Discrimination and Protection of Minorities, 50th Sess., E/CN.4/Sub.2/1998/13, 22 June 1998, para. 30, stating that '[i]n all respects and in all circumstances, sexual slavery is slavery and its prohibition is a jus cogens norm'.

[119] *Ntaganda* case (n 102), para. 52.

humanity'.[120] The Chamber not only stated that the prohibition of torture was a crime against humanity, but also held that the prohibition of torture is 'recognised in customary and conventional international law and as a norm of *jus cogens*'.[121] The International Criminal Court has similarly described the prohibition of crimes against humanity as *jus cogens*.[122]

In its judgment in the *East Timor* case, the International Court of Justice stated that the 'assertion that the *right of peoples to self-determination*, as it evolved from the Charter and from United Nations practice, has an *erga omnes* character, is irreproachable'.[123] It described the principle of self-determination as 'one of the essential principles of contemporary international law'.[124] Before the *East Timor* case, the Court had emphasized the importance of the right to self-determination in its advisory opinions on *Nambia* and *Western Sahara*.[125] The *erga omnes* character of the obligation to respect the right to self-determination was also recognized in the *Wall* advisory opinion.[126] Moreover, the Court applied the consequences of serious breaches of *jus cogens*—in particular the duty to cooperate to bring to an end a situation created by the breach—to the breach of the duty to respect the right to self-determination.[127]

The *jus cogens* status of *basic rules of international humanitarian law* has also been affirmed in the jurisprudence of international courts and tribunals. The International Court of Justice, in the *Nuclear Weapons* advisory opinion, considered the question of whether 'rules and principles

---

[120] *Prosecutor v Milan Simić*, IT-95-9/2-S, Sentencing Judgment, Trial Chamber, ICTY, 17 October 2002, para. 34.

[121] Ibid.

[122] See, e.g. *Prosecutor v William Samoei Ruto and Joshua Arap Sang*, ICC-01/09-01/11, Decision of Trial Chamber on the Request of Mr Ruto for Excusal from Continued Presence at Trial, International Criminal Court, 18 June 2013, para. 90 ('It is generally agreed that the interdiction of crimes against humanity enjoys the stature of *jus cogens*. In contrast, democracy as an international legal norm has not, so far, been known to enjoy the *jus cogens* status. Hence, in the event of any perceived conflict between the two norms, considerations of democracy must yield to the need to conduct proper inquiry into criminal responsibility of an elected official for crimes against humanity').

[123] *East Timor (Portugal v Australia)*, ICJ Reports 1995, p. 90, p. 102, para. 29.

[124] Ibid.

[125] See, generally, *Namibia* (n 49); *Western Sahara*, Advisory Opinion, ICJ Reports 1975, p. 12.

[126] *Legal Consequences of the Construction of the Wall in Occupied Palestinian Territory*, Advisory Opinion, ICJ Reports 2004, p. 136, especially at pp. 171–172, 196, paras 88, 149, and 155.

[127] Ibid., para. 159 ('[there is a duty on] all States ... to see to it that any impediment, resulting from the construction of the wall, to the exercise by the Palestinian people of its right to self-determination is brought to an end').

of humanitarian law' rose to the level of *jus cogens*.[128] Although the Court opted not to address the question directly, it did perhaps indirectly recognize the *jus cogens* status of some principles of international humanitarian law when it described these as 'intransgressible'. It does not signify rules that may not be violated, because all rules carry an obligation of compliance, including rules of a *jus dispositivum* character.[129]

Some individual opinions in the *Nuclear Weapons* advisory opinion did address the question of the *jus cogens* status of the rule directly.[130] Moreover, the *erga omnes* character of some rules of international humanitarian law was later proclaimed by the Court in its advisory opinion on the *Wall*.[131] Other courts and tribunals have been less tentative about the *jus cogens* nature of the basic rules of humanitarian law. In *Kupreškić*, the Trial Chamber of the ICTY stated that 'most norms of international humanitarian law', including in particular 'those prohibiting war crimes ... are also peremptory norms of international law or *jus cogens*, i.e. of a non-derogable and overriding character'.[132] Similarly, in the *Tadić* decision on the defence motion for interlocutory appeal on jurisdiction, the Tribunal's Appeals Chamber, in determining the applicable rules of international law, held that it may apply any treaty which was 'not in conflict with or derogating from peremptory norms of international law, as are most customary rules of international humanitarian law'.[133]

---

[128] *Legality of the Threat or Use of Nuclear Weapons* (n 111), p. 258, para. 83. See also *Corfu Channel* case, Judgment of 9 April 1949, ICJ Reports 1949, p. 4, at p. 22 ('Such obligations are based, not on the Hague Convention of 1907, No. VIII, which is applicable in time of war, but on certain general and well-recognized principles, namely: elementary considerations of humanity, even more exacting in peace than in war').

[129] See Christófolo (n 28) at p. 231.

[130] See, e.g. *Legality of the Threat or Use of Nuclear Weapons* (n 111), declaration of Judge Bedjaoui, at p. 273, para. 21 ('I have no doubt that most of the principles and rules of humanitarian law and, in any event, the two principles, one of which prohibits the use of weapons with indiscriminate effects and the other the use of arms causing unnecessary suffering, form part of *jus cogens*'); ibid., dissenting opinion of Judge Weeramantry, at p. 496 ('The rules of the humanitarian law of war have clearly acquired the status of *jus cogens*, for they are fundamental rules of a humanitarian character, from which no derogation is possible without negating the basic considerations of humanity which they are intended to protect'); ibid., dissenting opinion of Judge Koroma, at pp. 573 ff., see especially at p. 574, where Judge Koroma criticizes the Court for its 'judicial policy of "non-pronouncement"'.

[131] *Wall* (n 126), p. 199, para. 155 ('The obligations *erga omnes* violated by Israel are the obligation to respect the right of the Palestinian people to self-determination, and certain of its obligations under international humanitarian law').

[132] *Kupreškić* (n 84), para. 520.

[133] *Prosecutor v Dušan Tadić* et al., Case No. IT-94-1, Decision of the Appeals Chamber on the Defence Motion for Interlocutory Appeal on Jurisdiction, 2 October 1995, Judicial Reports 1994–1995, para. 143. See also *Prosecutor v Stanislav Galić*, Case No. IT-98-29-T, Judgment, Trial Chamber, ICTY, 5 December 2003, para. 98.

Finally, on the issue of hierarchy of norms, international and national tribunals have almost all avoided finding a conflict between international norms, probably to avoid having to conclude explicitly that one norm is superior to another. The *Jurisdictional Immunities of States* case began in December 2008, when the Federal Republic of Germany filed an application against Italy at the ICJ, asserting that the Italian courts' exercise of jurisdiction over Germany in relation to claims of World War II forced labour and other war crimes constituted a wrongful denial of sovereign immunity.[134] In its judgment of 3 February 2012, the Court held for Germany, first finding that 'there is almost no State practice which might be considered to support the proposition that a State is deprived of its entitlement to immunity' in a case of this type.[135] In addition, after reviewing treaty provisions, national legislation, and the judgments of national and international courts, the Court found that 'there is a substantial body of State practice from other countries which demonstrates that customary international law does not treat a State's entitlement to immunity as dependent upon the gravity of the act of which it is accused or the peremptory nature of the rule which it is alleged to have violated.'[136] Assuming without deciding that the alleged violations rose to the level of *jus cogens*, the Court held that there was no conflict between that determination and the rule demanding respect for sovereign immunity: 'the two sets of rules address different matters', one substantive, one procedural. There could be no conflict between the two.

Thus, because rules of immunities and possible *jus cogens* norms of the law of armed conflict 'address different matters', there was no conflict between them and States must continue to afford immunities under customary and treaty law.[137] There could be no conflict between immunity and *jus cogens* even in cases where 'a means by which a *jus cogens* rule might be enforced was rendered unavailable'.[138] A similar view of the relationship between *jus cogens* and procedural rules was adopted by the Court in *Armed Activities on the Territory of the Congo (DRC v Rwanda)*, where the Court found that even though the matter related to the *jus cogens* prohibition of genocide, this fact 'cannot of itself provide a basis for the jurisdiction of the

---

[134] *Jurisdictional Immunities of the State (Germany v Italy)*, ICJ, Application of 23 December 2008.

[135] Ibid., para. 80.

[136] Ibid, para. 84.

[137] *Jurisdictional Immunities of the State (Germany v Italy, Greece intervening)*, ICJ Merits, Judgment of 3 February 2012, paras 92, 95, and 97.

[138] *Jurisdictional Immunities of the State*, para. 95.

Court to entertain the dispute'.[139] These judgments suggest a narrow impact for *jus cogens* norms, limited only to acts directly related to the legality of the underlying conduct.

The *Arrest Warrant* case[140] involved the related question of official immunity for representatives of the State. The Court split into several divisions on the questions before it, with some judges expressing favour towards universal jurisdiction over war crimes or crimes against humanity, while other judges denied this competence for other States. One judge held there was no claim that the ICJ could decide within its jurisdiction, one dissent from the judgment, and one judge neutral on the issue of universal jurisdiction.[141] The Court held that a sitting Minister of Foreign Affairs enjoys full immunity from foreign jurisdictions even in the case of such serious allegations and that Belgium violated the rights of the DRC when it issued an arrest warrant for the foreign minister. Belgium argued that immunities such as those claimed in this case do not apply when the accusations involve war crimes or crimes against humanity. The Court held there is no such exception in customary international law. The three favouring universal jurisdiction see a trend to provide in international law for the trial and punishment of those who have committed certain crimes extraterritorially, but noted the cautious approach of most national courts. In fact, no jurisprudence was available for a trial in absentia for offences such as those alleged in this case. There is, therefore, no international custom permitting Belgium to exercise jurisdiction in this matter, but none establishing that it is prohibited either. 'In short, national legislation and case law—that is, State practice—is neutral as to the exercise of universal jurisdiction.'[142] Nonetheless, there are 'certain indications' that jurisdiction based on the heinous nature of the crimes committed, is not unlawful, citing the Geneva Conventions in support. Thus, prosecuting the Minister of Foreign Affairs for the crimes he allegedly committed would be within that small category of acts in respect

[139] *Armed Activities on the Territory of the Congo*, at para. 64.

[140] Case *Concerning the Arrest Warrant of 11 April 2000 (DRC v Belgium)* ICJ, 14 February 2002.

[141] Judge Oda argued the ICJ lacked jurisdiction; Judges Buergenthal, Higgens, and Kooijmans expressed the view in favour of universal jurisdiction; Guillaume, Rezek, and Ranjeva opposed this view. Koroma was somewhat neutral on the issue, although he did express his opinion that universal jurisdiction is available for piracy, war crimes, and crimes against humanity, such as slave trading and genocide. In his view, however, the Court was not obliged to take a position on this question. Judge Al-Khasawneh and Judge *ad hoc* Van den Wyngaert dissented on the finding of a violation by Belgium of its duty to respect the immunity of the foreign minister. In all, there were nine separate opinions in the case.

[142] *Arrest Warrant* case, Separate opinion of Judges Higgins, Kooijmans, and Buergenthal.

of which an exercise of universal jurisdiction is not precluded under international law. All this without pronouncing the term jus cogens.

b. Jurisprudence of regional courts and tribunals

Regional tribunals have also pronounced on many of the norms cited by the fourth report as norms *jus cogens*. The case of *Yassin Abdullah Kadi and Al Barakaat International Foundation v Council of the European Union and Commission of the European Communities* (joined cases C-402/05 P and C-415/05 P; hereinafter 'the *Kadi* judgment') concerned the freezing of the applicants' assets pursuant to European Community regulations adopted in connection with the implementation of Security Council resolutions 1267 (1999), 1333 (2000), and 1390 (2002), which, among other things, required all UN member States to take measures to freeze the funds and other financial resources of the individuals and entities identified by the Security Council's Sanctions Committee as being associated with Osama bin Laden, al-Qaeda, or the Taliban. In that case the applicants fell within that category and their assets had thus been frozen contrary to their right to property. They contended that the EC regulations had been adopted *ultra vires*.

On 21 September 2005 the Court of First Instance (after December 1, 2009 known as the General Court) rejected those complaints and confirmed the lawfulness of the regulations, finding mainly that Article 103 of the Charter had the effect of placing Security Council resolutions above all other international obligations (except for those covered by *jus cogens*), including those arising from the EC treaty. It concluded that it was not entitled to review Security Council resolutions, even on an incidental basis, to ascertain whether they respected fundamental rights.

Mr Kadi appealed to the Court of Justice of the European Union (CJEC) (after 1 December 2009). A Grand Chamber examined the appeal jointly with another case. In its judgment of 3 September 2008, the CJEC found that, in view of the internal and autonomous nature of the Community legal order, it had jurisdiction to review the lawfulness of a Community regulation adopted within the ambit of that order, even if its purpose was to implement a Security Council resolution. It thus held that it was entitled to review Community acts or acts of member States designed to give effect to such resolutions, and that this 'would not entail any challenge to the primacy of that resolution in international law'. The CJEC concluded that the Community judiciary had to ensure the full review of the lawfulness of all Community acts in the light of the fundamental rights forming an integral part of the general principles of Community law, including review of Community measures which, like the contested regulation, were designed to give effect to resolutions of the Security Council.

The European Court of Human Rights (ECtHR) has pronounced the prohibition of genocide to be a norm *jus cogens*. In the case of *Jorgic v Germany*,[143] the applicant, an ethnic Serb national of Bosnia and Herzegovina, entered Germany in 1969 and legally resided there until the beginning of 1992. He then returned to Bosnia, where he was born. He remained there until 16 December 1995 when he was arrested entering Germany and placed in pre-trial detention on the ground that he was strongly suspected of having committed acts of genocide. He was convicted of genocide by the Düsseldorf Court of Appeal, a conviction upheld by the Federal Court of Justice and the Federal Constitutional Court. He alleged that the courts had no jurisdiction over his case, and his ensuing detention thus amounted to a violation of Article 5 § 1(a) and Article 6 § 1 of the Convention.

Article 6 no. 1 of the Criminal Code, taken in conjunction with Article 220a of that Code then in force provided that German criminal law was applicable and that, consequently, German courts had jurisdiction to try persons charged with genocide committed abroad, regardless of the defendant's and the victims' nationalities. The domestic courts had therefore established jurisdiction in accordance with the clear wording of the pertinent provisions of the Criminal Code. However, the European Court also had to ascertain whether the domestic courts' decision was equally in compliance with the provisions of public international law, based on the principle of universal jurisdiction as confronted with the public international law duty of non-intervention. In the German courts' view, the principle of universal jurisdiction was not excluded by the wording of Article VI of the Genocide Convention. That article was to be understood as establishing a duty for the courts named therein to try persons suspected of genocide, while not prohibiting the prosecution of genocide by other national courts.

In determining whether the domestic courts' interpretation of the applicable rules of public international law on jurisdiction was reasonable, the ECtHR observed that the Contracting Parties to the Genocide Convention

---

[143] *Jorgic v Germany*, App. 74613/01, Judgment (Merits) of 12 December 2007.

had not agreed to codify the principle of universal jurisdiction over genocide, but nonetheless pursuant to Genocide Convention Article I, the Contracting Parties were under an *erga omnes* obligation to prevent and punish genocide, the prohibition of which forms part of the *jus cogens*. In view of this, the national courts' reasoning that the purpose of the Genocide Convention, as expressed notably in that Article, did not exclude jurisdiction for the punishment of genocide by States whose laws establish extraterritoriality in this respect must be considered as reasonable (and indeed convincing). The European Court thus concluded that the German courts' interpretation of the applicable provisions and rules of public international law was not arbitrary. They therefore had reasonable grounds for establishing their jurisdiction to try the applicant on charges of genocide. It followed that the applicant's case was heard by a tribunal established by law within the meaning of Article 6 § 1 of the Convention. There has therefore been no violation of that provision.

Regional courts have consistently held that the prohibition of torture is a norm of *jus cogens*. In *Espinoza Gonzáles v Peru,* for example, the Inter-American Court made the following observations concerning torture:

> The prohibition of torture and cruel, inhuman or degrading treatment or punishment is absolute and non-derogable, even under the most difficult circumstances, such as war, threat of war, the fight against terrorism and any other crimes, states of emergency, or internal unrest or conflict, suspension of constitutional guarantees, internal political instability or other public emergencies or catastrophes. Nowadays, this prohibition is part of international *jus cogens*.[144]

The Court first itself recognized the prohibition of torture as *jus cogens* in 2000, in *Bámaca-Velásquez v Guatemala*.[145] This position has been reiterated and confirmed in many subsequent judgments of the Inter-American Court.[146] This consistent jurisprudence has been affirmed by

---

[144] *Espinoza Gonzáles v Peru*, Judgment (Preliminary objections, merits, reparations and costs), IACtHR, 20 November 2014, Series C, No. 289, para. 141.

[145] *Bámaca-Velásquez v Guatemala*, Judgment (Merits), IACtHR, 25 November 2000,

[146] See, e.g. *La Cantuta v Peru*, IACtHR, Merits, Reparations, and Costs, Series C No. 162, Judgment of 29 November 2006, para. 160. 'As pointed out repeatedly, the acts involved in the instant case have violated peremptory norms of international law (*jus cogens*). Under Article 1(1) of the American Convention, the States have the duty to investigate human rights violations and to prosecute and punish those responsible. In view of the nature and seriousness of the events, all the more since the context of this case is one of systematic violation of human rights, the need to eradicate impunity reveals itself to the international community as a duty of

the Inter-American Commission on Human Rights in, for example, *Ortiz Hernandez v Venezuela*.[147]

It has consistently held that the prohibition of torture is a norm of *jus cogens*.

Like the Inter-American Court,[148] the European Court of Human Rights has been unequivocal in recognizing the *jus cogens* character of the *prohibition against torture*. In *Al-Adsani v the United Kingdom*, a case often referred to as an authority for the view that there are no exceptions to immunity even for *jus cogens* violations, the Court, having surveyed international practice, 'accepts, on the basis of [that practice], that the prohibition of torture has achieved the status of a peremptory norm in international law'.[149] Similarly, in the *Jones v the United Kingdom* case, the Court proceeded from the assumption that the prohibition of torture is *jus cogens* and upheld, in all material respects, the *Al-Adsani* case.[150] The African Commission on Human and Peoples' Rights has likewise recognized, in

cooperation among states for such purpose. Access to justice constitutes a peremptory norm of International Law and, as such, it gives rise to the States' *erga omnes* obligation to adopt all such measures as are necessary to prevent such violations from going unpunished, whether exercising their judicial power to apply their domestic law and International Law to judge and eventually punish those responsible for such events, or collaborating with other States aiming in that direction. The Court points out that, under the collective guarantee mechanism set out in the American Convention, and the regional and universal obligations in this regard, the States Parties to the Convention must collaborate with one another towards that end.'

[147] *Johan Alexis Ortiz Hernández v Venezuela*, Case 12.270, Report of the Inter-American Commission on Human Rights, Report No. 2/15 of 29 January 2015, para. 212. See also *Omar Maldonado Vargas, Alvaro Yánez del Villar, Mario Antonio Cornejo* et al. *v Chile*, Case 12.500, Report of the IACHR, Report No. 119/13 of 8 November 2013; *Cosme Rosa Genoveva, Evandro de Oliveira and Others v Brazil*, Cases 11.566 and 11.694, Report of the IACHR, Report No. 141/11 of 31 October 2011, para. 167.

[148] See, e.g. *Mendoza* et al. *v Argentina*, Judgment (Preliminary objections, merits and reparations), IACtHR, 14 May 2013, Series C, No. 260, para. 199 ('the Court reiterates its case law to the effect that, today, the absolute prohibition of torture, both physical and mental, is part of international *jus cogens*'); *Case of the Massacres of El Mozote and Nearby Places v El Salvador*, Judgment (Merits, Reparations and Costs), IACtHR, 25 October 2012, Series C, No. 252; *The Barrios Family v Venezuela*, Judgment (Merits, Reparations and Costs), IACtHR, 24 November 2011, Series C, No. 237, para. 50; *Case of the 'Las Dos Erres' Massacre v Guatemala*, Judgment (Preliminary Objection, Merits, Reparations, and Costs), IACtHR, 24 November 2009, Series C, No. 211.

[149] *Al-Adsani v the United Kingdom*, No. 35763/91, Judgment, Grand Chamber, ECtHR, 21 November 2001, ECHR 2001-XI, para. 61.

[150] *Jones and Others v the United Kingdom*, No. 34356/06 and 40528/06, Judgment, ECtHR, 14 January 2014, ECHR 2014, especially paras 205–215. See also *A v The Netherlands*, No. 4900/06, Judgment, ECtHR, 20 July 2010, para. 133, holding that 'the rule prohibiting expulsion to face torture or ill-treatment ... had arguably also attained the status of *ius cogens*, meaning that it had become a peremptory, non-derogable norm of international law'.

Mohammed Abdullah Saleh al-Asad v Djibouti, the prohibition of torture as a norm of *jus cogens*.[151]

In the *Council of the European Union v Front populaire pour la libération de la saguia-el-hamra et du rio de oro,* the Grand Chamber of the European Court of Justice described the right to self-determination as a principle of international law that is a 'legally enforceable right *erga omnes* and one of the essential principles of international law'.[152] The African Commission on Human and Peoples' Rights has also affirmed the fundamental importance of the right to self-determination.[153]

In other regional cases, only concurring judges referred to *jus cogens*. In the European Court case of *Jamaa Hirsi and Others v Italy*,[154] the separate opinion of Judge Pinto de Albuqurque found non-refoulement to be a *jus cogens* norm, citing the Inter-American Court's Advisory Opinion OC-18-03 on the juridical condition and rights of undocumented migrants, issued 17 September 2003. In that opinion, the Inter-American Court affirmed the fundamental principle that 'non-discrimination and the right of equality are *jus cogens* applicable to all residents regardless of immigration status'.[155]

The peremptory status of the *prohibition against slavery* has also been recognized in decisions of regional courts, in particular by the Inter-American Court. In *Río Negro Massacres v Guatemala*, the Court held that the failure to investigate and prosecute 'slavery and involuntary servitude' contravened 'non-derogable norms (*jus cogens*)'.[156] In *Aloeboetoe v Suriname*, the Inter-American Court held that a treaty between the Netherlands and the Saramakas community providing for the transport of slaves would be 'null and void'.[157] In the reparations phase of the case, the Commission

---

[151] *Mohammed Abdullah Saleh al-Asad v the Republic of Djibouti*, Communication 383/10, Decision of April–May 2014, para. 179 ('The prohibition of torture is a *jus cogens* rule of international law').

[152] *Council of the European Union v Front populaire pour la libération de la saguia-el-hamra et du rio de oro (Front Polisario)*, Case C-104/16 P, Judgment, Grand Chamber, European Court of Justice, 21 December 2016, *Official Journal of the European Union*, C 53/19 (20 February 2017), para. 88.

[153] *Congrès du peuple katangais v DRC*, Communication 75/92, Decision, African Commission on Human and Peoples' Rights, para. 4, and *Kevin Mgwanga Gunme* et al. *v Cameroon*, Communication 266/03, Decision, African Commission on Human and Peoples' Rights. In both cases, the Commission stressed that the right could be exercised in ways other than secession.

[154] *Jamaa Hirsi and Others v Italy*, App. No. 27765/09, Judgment of 23 February 2012, (Merits and Just Satisfaction) (Grand Chamber).

[155] *Juridical Condition and Rights of the Undocumented Migrants*, IACtHR, Advisory Opinion, Series A No. 18, 17 September 2003, at 95–96.

[156] *Rio Negro Massacres*, at para. 227.

[157] *Aloeboetoe and others v Suriname*, IACtHR, Reparations and Costs, Series C No. 15, Judgment of 10 September 1993.

argued the applicability of a treaty dated 19 September 1762 between the Saramakas and the Dutch authorities, according to which the Saramakas were granted internal autonomy and rights over their own territory, both of which were relevant to the issue of reparations.[158] The Court held that it was unnecessary to inquire as to whether or not an agreement between an indigenous group and a state is an international treaty, because 'even if that were the case, the treaty would today be null and void because it contradicts the norms of *jus cogens superveniens*'.

The Court seemed to conclude that the entire treaty would be void and not simply the two provisions concerning slavery that it cited as violating *jus cogens*. The fact of having provisions upholding slavery was enough for the Court: 'No treaty of that nature may be invoked before an international human rights tribunal'.[159] The Inter-American Court's view in *Aloeboetoe* seems supported by the language of Article 53 VCLT, which refers only to the nullity *ab initio* of a treaty that conflicts with a norm of *jus cogens*.[160] The commentary to the fourth report also makes clear the view of the Special Rapporteur that a single illegal provision does not entail the nullity of the treaty as a whole if the provision is severable and the objective of the treaty as a whole can be upheld. During the drafting of the Vienna Convention on the Law of Treaties, Waldock's more expansive provision on treaties void for illegality similarly contained a paragraph that allowed for declaring invalid as contrary to *jus cogens* a provision clearly severable and 'not essentially connected with the principal objects'.[161] Although the paragraph was not retained in the VCLT, it may be implicit in the version adopted.

The jurisprudence in the Inter-American System has also described the *prohibition of crimes against humanity* as having peremptory status. In *Miguel Castro-Castro Prison v Peru*, the Inter-American Court of Human Rights determined that the prohibition of crimes against humanity was part of peremptory norms of general international law.[162] The *Miguel Castro-Castro Prison* judgment was itself based on *Almonacid-Arellano v*

---

[158] Ibid., para. 56.

[159] Ibid, para. 57.

[160] H. Lauterpacht, Special Rapporteur, Report on the Law of Treaties: Legality of the object of the treaty, 5th sess. of the ILC, UN Doc. A/CN.4/63, 24 March 1953, Art. 15, at 154 (emphasis added).

[161] Sir H. Waldock, Special Rapporteur, Second report on the Law of Treaties: Treaties void for illegality. 15th sess. of the ILC, UN Doc. A/CN.4/156 and Add.1-3, 1963, Article 13(3), at 52.

[162] *Miguel Castro-Castro Prison v Peru*, Judgment (Merits, Reparations, and Costs), IACtHR, 25 November 2006, para. 402.

Chile, which concluded that the prohibition of crimes against humanity was a norm of *jus cogens* after an assessment of practice starting with the Nuremberg Principles.[163] The Inter-American Commission has similarly affirmed the *jus cogens* status of the prohibition of crimes against humanity.[164]

Overall, the Inter-American Court has been the most active international court in announcing norms to be *jus cogens*. It also seems that only the Inter-American Court has suggested the possibility of practical functions or consequences resulting from violation of a *jus cogens* norm, results that may lead to regional judgments inconsistent with those of the ICJ and the European Court in respect to immunities. In the *La Cantuta* case, the Court referred to the duty of all states in the system to cooperate in bringing to justice those individuals who were responsible for violating the *jus cogens* norm prohibiting forced disappearances.[165] The Court called the duty to prosecute and punish these crimes a *jus cogens* duty, which would directly conflict with norms on immunities. Second, the Court has referred to the concept of aggravated violations giving rise to enhanced reparations, a concept it is likely to apply in the context of *jus cogens* violations.[166]

The Inter-American Court of Human Rights also referred to *jus cogens* in its 2003 advisory opinion on migrant workers, which discussed the legal status of the principle of non-discrimination and the right to equal protection of the law. According to the Court, '[a]ll persons have attributes inherent to their human dignity that may not be harmed; these attributes make them possessors of fundamental rights that may not be disregarded

---

[163] *Almonacid-Arellano and Others v Chile*, Judgment (Preliminary Objections, Merits and Costs), IACtHR, 26 September 2006, Series C, No. 154, para. 99. See also IACtHR, *Goiburú and Others (Merits, Reparations, and Costs)*, Judgment of 22 September 2006, Ser. C, No. 153., para. 128, which described the prohibition of torture and enforced disappearance as crimes against humanity and *jus cogens*. See further *Manuel Cepeda Vargas v Colombia*, Judgment (Preliminary Objections, Merits, Reparations, and Costs), IACtHR, 26 May 2010, Series C, No. 213, para. 42.

[164] See, e.g. *Manuel Cepeda Vargas v Republic of Colombia*, Case 12.531, Decision, IACHR, 14 November 2008, footnote 66; *Julia Gomes Lund and Others (Guerrilha do Araguaia) v Brazil*, Case 11.552, Decision, IACHR, 26 March 2009, para. 185 (duty to investigate and prosecute crimes against humanity described as *jus cogens*); *Juan Gelman and Others v Uruguay*, Case 12.607, Decision, IACHR, 21 January 2010, para. 66; *Marino Lopez and Others (Operation Genesis) v Colombia*, Case 12.573, Merits, Decision, IACHR, 31 March 2011, Report No. 64/11, para. 256, at footnote 275.

[165] IACtHR, *La Cantuta* case (n 146).

[166] First discussed in the *Myrna Mack Chang* case, this notion of aggravated violations has been repeatedly cited in the IACtHR. *Myrna Mack-Chang Case*, IACtHR, Merits, Reparations, and Costs, Series C No. 101, Judgment of 25 November 2003.

and which are, consequently, superior to the power of the State, whatever its political structure'.[167]

The Court concluded that non-discrimination is *jus cogens*, being 'intrinsically related to the right to equal protection before the law', which, in turn, derives 'directly from the oneness of the human family and is linked to the essential dignity of the individual'. The Court added that the principle belongs to *jus cogens* because the whole legal structure of national and international public order rests on it and it is a fundamental principle that permeates all laws. The Court's opinion considerably shifts lawmaking from States to international tribunals, as the latter assess the demands of human dignity and international public order to elevate particular norms to peremptory status.

The Court has also affirmed *jus cogens* norms in contentious cases, not only to include the prohibition of torture,[168] but also the right of access to justice, the prohibition of forced disappearance, and the duty to prosecute violations of *jus cogens* norms.[169] In its own jurisprudence, the

---

[167] In stating that *jus cogens* has been developed by international case law, the Court cited two judgments of the ICJ, although neither of them discusses the subject, namely *Application of the Convention on the Prevention and Punishment of the Crime of Genocide, Preliminary Objections (Bosnia-Herzegovina v Yugoslavia)*, ICJ, Preliminary objections, Judgment of 11 July 1996, at 595; and *Barcelona Traction* (n 93), at 3.

[168] See the following Inter-American Court of Human Rights cases: *Bayarri v Argentina*, IACtHR, Preliminary Objection, Merits, Reparations, and Costs, Series C No. 187, Judgment of 30 October 2008, para. 81; *Martiza Urrutia v Guatemala*, IACtHR, Merits, Reparations, and Costs, Series C No. 103, Judgment of 27 November 2003, para. 92; *Tibi v Ecuador*, IACtHR, Preliminary Objections, Merits, Reparations, and Costs, Series C No. 114, Judgment of 7 September 2004, para. 143; *Bueno-Alves v Argentina*, IACtHR, Merits, Reparations, and Costs, Series C No. 164, Judgment of 11 May 2007, para. 76; *Case of the Rochela Massacre v Colombia*, IACtHR, Merits, Reparations, and Costs, Series C No. 163, Judgment of 11 May 2007, para. 132; *Case of the Miguel Castro-Castro Prison v Peru*, IACtHR, Merits, Reparations, and Costs, Series C No. 160, Judgment of 25 November 2006, para. 271.

[169] Ibid., para. 157. See also *Ríos et al. v Venezuela*, IACtHR, Preliminary Objections, Merits, Reparations, and Costs, Series C No. 194, Judgment of 28 January 2009; *Tiu-Tojín v Guatemala*, IACtHR, Merits, Reparations, and Costs, Series C No. 190, Judgment of 26 November 2008. '[W]e should reiterate to the State that the prohibition of the forced disappearance of persons and the related duty to investigate them and, if it were the case, punish those responsible has the nature of *jus cogens*. As such, the forced disappearance of persons cannot be considered a political crime or related to political crimes under any circumstance, to the effect of preventing the criminal persecution of this type of crimes or suppressing the effects of a conviction. Additionally, pursuant with the preamble of the Inter-American Convention on Forced Disappearance, the systematic practice of the forced disappearance of persons constitutes a crime against humanity and, as such, entails the consequences established in the applicable international law'. *Tiu-Tojín v Guatemala*, para. 91. See also *Perozo et al. v Venezuela*, IACtHR, Preliminary Objections, Merits, Reparations, and Costs, Series C No. 195, Judgment of 28 January 2009, para. 157 (citing *La Cantuta v Peru* (n 146)).

Inter-American Commission on Human Rights has declared the right to life to be a norm of *jus cogens*, invoking natural law traditions

> derived from a higher order of norms established in ancient times and which cannot be contravened by the laws of man or nations. The norms of *jus cogens* have been described by public law specialists as those which encompass public international order ... accepted ... as necessary to protect the public interest of the society of nations or to maintain levels of public morality recognized by them.[170]

In each of the cases, the declaration of *jus cogens* appears to have little or no practical consequence. All the norms cited are extensively found in treaty law and probably constitute customary international law as well. Thus, any contrary domestic law or practice contravenes international law and Inter-American agreements. One commentator has speculated that the Inter-American System's frequent invocation of *jus cogens* is in part due to the fact that its cases generally have concerned gross and systematic violations of non-derogable rights and that each judgment 'est pour elle une opportunité de rappeler avec fermeté aux gouvernements l'importance du respect de la dignité et des droits de la personne humaine'.[171] As noted earlier, it can also be attributed in part to the theories of one judge whose views resonated with a strong tradition of natural law in Latin America. The pronouncements on *jus cogens* have largely diminished with changes in the composition of the Court.

5.3 National Legislation and Jurisprudence

National legislatures[172] and courts have also reflected the declaratory function of *jus cogens*, expressing that this particular norm is one taken very

---

[170] *Victims of the Tugboat '13 de Marzo' v Cuba*, IACHR, Case 11.436, Report No. 47/96, OEA/Ser.L/V/II.95 Doc. 7 rev., 1997, at 146–147.

[171] C. Maia, 2009, 'Le *jus cogens* dans la jurisprudence de la Cour interaméricaine des droits de l'homme', in L. Hennebel and H. Tigroudja (eds), *Le particularisme interaméricain des droits de l'homme* (Paris, Pedone), p. 277.

[172] See, for a comprehensive list of national legislation prohibiting torture, Association for the Prevention of Torture, Compilation of Torture Laws, http://tortureprevention.ch/en/compilation-of-torture-laws/ (accessed on 3 September 2020). See, for random examples of legislation prohibiting torture in absolute terms: sect. 25 of the Constitution, sects. 74, 86, and 87 of the Criminal Code, sect. 5 of the Criminal Procedure Code (Albania); arts 34 and 132 of the Constitution and arts 263 *bis, ter, quater* of the Penal Code (Algeria); sect. 274 of the Criminal Code Act (Australia); Art. 5 of the Constitution (Brazil); Art. 38 of the Constitution

seriously in law and policy. Domestic court cases generally fall into one of two categories. First are cases in which sovereign immunity has acted to shield defendants from civil lawsuits for damages.[173] The issue has arisen most often in courts of the United States[174] and the United Kingdom.[175] In both forums, lawyers have argued that the foreign sovereign immunity must be interpreted to include an implied exception to sovereign immunity for violations of *jus cogens* norms. Nearly every court thus far has rejected the argument and upheld immunity, although some judicial panels have split on the issue.

The second category of domestic law cases in which the nature of norms as *jus cogens* has been asserted are cases filed pursuant to the US Alien Tort Claim Act (ATCA).[176] Some of the plaintiffs assert violations of norms *jus cogens*,[177] but no ATCA case has turned on the character of the norm as *jus cogens* instead of custom. Moreover, most of the cases have been decided as default judgments, the defendants not appearing to contest the suits; enforcement has also proved difficult, as most of the defendants lacked assets in the United States. One dangerous consequence of repeatedly pleading

---

(Cambodia); Art. 259A of the Penal Code (Czech Republic); sect. 157A of the Civil Criminal Code, sects 10A and 27A of the Military Criminal Code (Denmark); sect. 44 of the Constitution (Iceland); Art. 401 of the Criminal Code (Lebanon); art. 36 of the Constitution, Art. 486 of the Penal Code, Art. 227 of the Criminal Procedure Code (Malta); Art. 31 of the Constitution (Kuwait).

[173] See, e.g. *Bouzari v Iran*, [2004] 71 O.R.3d 675 (Can.) (holding that the prohibition against torture does not entail a right to a civil remedy enforceable in a foreign court). With respect to national court decisions, in *Jurisdictional Immunities of the State* the Court cited decisions in Canada, Greece, New Zealand, Poland, Slovenia, and the United Kingdom where sovereign immunity was acknowledged, even in the face of allegations of *jus cogens* violations. *Jurisdictional Immunities of the State*, para. 96.

[174] For the United States, intermediate courts have rejected an implied exception to sovereign immunity where the foreign State was accused of violating *jus cogens* norms. See *Siderman de Blake v Argentina*; *Princz v Germany*, 26 F.3d 1166 (D.C. Cir. 1994); *Smith v Libya*, 101 F.3d 239 (2d Cir. 1997; and *Sampson v Germany*, 250 F.3d 1145, (7th Cir. 2001). For immunity of officials, see *Ye v Zemin*, 383 F.3d 620, (7th Cir. 2004), at 625–627. Contrast *Giraldo v Drummond Co.*, 493 Fed. Appx. 106 (D.C. Cir. 2012) (acknowledging immunity of foreign government officials despite allegations of *jus cogens* violations), with *Yousuf v Samantar*, USSC, No. 08–1555, 1 June 2010.

[175] *Al-Adsani v. Kuwait* was litigated in English courts before it was submitted to the ECtHR. For the Court of Appeal's judgment, see *Al-Adsani v Government of Kuwait (No. 2)* (1996) 107 ILR 536.

[176] 'The [federal] district courts shall have original jurisdiction of any civil action by an alien for a tort only, committed in violation of the law of nations or a treaty of the United States'. Judiciary Act of 1789, ch. 20, § 9(b) (1789), codified at 28 USC § 1350.

[177] *Filartiga v Peña-Irala*, 630 F.2d 876 (2nd Cir. 1980). The United States Supreme Court decisions arising under the ATCA, including *Sosa v Alvarez-Machain*, 542 US 692 (2004), reprinted in (2004) 43 ILM 1390, do not mention *jus cogens*.

jus cogens in domestic cases may be emerging in US cases, where lawyers comment privately that some judges now only respond to pleas of *jus cogens* and discount customary international law, relegating it to a status akin to comity.

Some national courts have identified the prohibition of aggression as a norm *jus cogens*.[178] The decision of the German Federal Administrative Court concerning discipline of a person who had refused to comply with an order in respect of the war in Iraq that was deemed to be illegal is noteworthy.[179] There, the Court stated that '[i]nternational *ius cogens* includes *inter alia* the international prohibition of the use of force, as reflected in Article 2 (4) of the Charter of the United Nations'.[180]

The recognition of the prohibition of torture as a norm of jus cogens has also been ubiquitous in the decisions of national courts.[181] In Australia, the

---

[178] *A v Federal Department of Economic Affairs*, Judgment of the Swiss Federal Supreme Court of 23 January 2008, ILCD 1200 (CH 2008), para. 8.2 ('A titre d'exemple, on cite généralement les normes ayant trait à l'interdiction du recours à la force' [As an example, we can generally cite the norms concerning the prohibition of the recourse to force]); *Committee of US Citizens Living in Nicaragua and Others v President Reagan and Others*, 859 F2d 929, at 941; *RM v Attorney-General*, Judgment, High Court of Kenya, 1 December 2006, *ILDC* 699 (KE 2006), para. 42.

[179] *Federal Administrative Court*, Order of 21 June 2005, BVerwG 2 WD 12.04.

[180] Ibid.

[181] See, e.g. *Bouzari v Islamic Republic of Iran and the Attorney-General of Canada*, Judgment, Court of Appeal for Ontario, Canada, 30 June 2004, para. 36 ('First, the action is based on torture by a foreign State, which is a violation of both international human rights and peremptory norms of public international law'); *Lydienne X Prosecutor*, Appeal Judgment, Court of Cassation of France (Criminal Division), 19 March 2013, *ILDC* 2035 (FR2013), para. 10.4 ('l'interdiction de la torture a valeur de norme imperative ou *jus cogens* en droit international, laquelle prime les autres règles du droit international et constitue une restriction légitime á l'immunité de jurisdiction.' [the prohibition of torture is of an imperative nature or *jus cogens*, which takes precedence over other rules of international law and constitutes a legitimate restriction of immunity from jurisdiction]); *Lozano v Italy*, Judgment, Italian Court of Cassation (First Criminal Chamber), 24 July 2008, ILDC 1085, para. 6.; *S v Mthembu*, Judgment, South African Supreme Court of Appeal, 10 April 2008, para. 31 ('The [Convention against Torture] prohibits torture in absolute terms and no derogation from it is permissible, even in the event of a public emergency. It is thus a peremptory norm of international law'); See, e.g. *Committee of US Citizens Living in Nicaragua and Others v Reagan* (n 178), para. 56; *Siderman de Blake v Argentina*, Judgment, United States Court of Appeal, Ninth Circuit, at 714 ('we agree with the Sidermans that official acts of torture of the sort they allege Argentina to have committed constitute a *jus cogens* violation'); *Yousuf v Samantar*, Judgment, United States Court of Appeal, Fourth Circuit, at 19; *Belhaj v Straw; Rahmatullah v Minister of Defence*, Judgment, United Kingdom Supreme Court, 17 January 2017, especially opinion of Lord Sumption, at 717, ('The prohibition has the status of *jus cogens erga omnes*. That is to say that it is a peremptory norm of international law which gives rise to obligations owed by each state to all other states and from which no derogation can be justified by any countervailing public interest'); *Jones and Others v Ministry of Interior of Saudi Arabia*, Judgment, House of Lords of the UK, 14 June 2006, paras 43 and 44 ('there is no doubt that the prohibition on torture is such a norm [of *jus cogens*] ... The *jus cogens* is the prohibition on torture').

Federal Court, in Habib v the Commonwealth of Australia, recognized that the prohibition of torture is 'a peremptory norm of international law from which no derogation is permitted'.[182]

The peremptory character of the prohibition of apartheid and racial discrimination has also been recognized in judicial decisions of national courts. For example, racial discrimination and inequality was recognized as one of the examples of norms of *jus cogens* in the Swiss case *A v Department of Economic Affairs*.[183] Similarly, the United States Court of Appeals in *Committee of US Citizens Living in Nicaragua*, included racial discrimination in the list of norms of *jus cogens*.[184] In *Sarei v Rio Tinto*, the United States Court of Appeal stated that there was 'a great deal of support for the proposition that systematic racial discrimination by a State violates a *jus cogens* norm'.[185] National court cases have also recognized the prohibition of slavery as a norm of *jus cogens*.[186]

There is State practice recognizing and accepting the prohibition of genocide as a norm of *jus cogens*, including domestic court decisions. The prohibition of genocide was, for example, recognized as such by the Swiss Federal Court in *A v Federal Department of Economic Affairs*.[187] Similarly, in *RM v Attorney-General*, the High Court of Kenya, denying the *jus cogens* status of the prohibition of discrimination against children born out of wedlock (and their mothers), included the prohibition of genocide in its list of norms that did qualify as *jus cogens*.[188] The German Constitutional Court, in the case concerning an appeal in relation to a conviction of a Bosnian-Serb for acts of genocide, relied on the International Court of Justice's finding that the prohibition of genocide constituted an *erga omnes* obligation and a norm of *jus cogens*.[189] The Canadian Court of Appeal, in *R v Munyaneza*, a case concerning a Rwandan national implicated in the commission of genocide in Rwanda in 1994, determined that 'the crime of

---

[182] *Mamdouh Habib v the Commonwealth of Australia*, Judgment, Federal Court of Australia, 25 February 2010 [2010] FCAFC 1518, para. 9.

[183] *A v Federal Department of Economic Affairs* (n 178), para. 8.2.

[184] *Committee of US Citizens Living in Nicaragua* (n 178), at 941.

[185] *Sarei and Others v Rio Tinto, PLC*, Judgment, United States Court of Appeals for the Ninth District, 25 October 2011, at 19360.

[186] *Okenyo v Attorney General*, Judgment of the 29 March 2012, para. 61.

[187] *A v Federal Department of Economic Affairs* (n 178).

[188] *RM v Attorney-Genera and Four Othersl*, Judgment, High Court of Kenya, 1 December 2006, [2006] *EKL*. Petition 705 of 2007 in the matter of section 84(1) of the Constitution of Kenya [2006] AHRLR 256.

[189] *Beschluss der 4. Kammer des Zweiten Senats vom 12. Dezember 2000* [Federal Constitutional Court Order of 12 December 2000], 2 BVR 1290/90.

genocide in 1994 was in contravention of all the peremptory rules of customary international law'.[190] The United States Court of Appeal, in *Sarei v Rio Tinto*, also held that 'the status of genocide as a *jus cogens* norm remains indisputable'.[191]

The *jus cogens* status of the right to self-determination has also been affirmed in national court decisions. The German Constitutional Court, for example, included the right to self-determination as a rule of *jus cogens*, describing the latter as 'rules of law which are firmly rooted in the legal conviction of the community of States'.[192]

The peremptory status of the prohibition of crimes against humanity has also been affirmed in the decisions of national courts. In the United States, the District Court for the Eastern District of New York stated that the prohibition of crimes against humanity has 'existed in customary international law for over half a century', and is 'also deemed to be part of jus cogens—the highest standing in international legal norms'.[193] The Supreme Court of Argentina, in the *Mazzeo, Julio Lilo* case, described *jus cogens* as the highest international law imposed on States, noting that it 'prohibits the commission of crimes against humanity, even during times of war'.[194] In other jurisdictions it has been held that rules relating to the punishment of crimes against humanity, such as the inapplicability of prescription and the duty to prevent and punish, constitute peremptory norms of international law.[195] Similarly, the South African Constitutional Court's judgment in the *National Commissioner of Police v Southern African Litigation Centre* appears to endorse the *jus cogens* status of the prohibition:

---

[190] *R v Munyaneza*, Judgment, Superior Court (Criminal Division) of Canada, 22 May 2009, para. 75.

[191] *Sarei and Others v Rio Tinto, PLC* (n 185).

[192] Federal Constitutional Court Order of 26 October 2004—2 BVR 1038/01. See also *Saharawi Arab Democratic Republic and Others v Cherry Blossom and Others*, Judgment of the High Court of South Africa of 15 June 2016, especially at para. 39 ff.

[193] In *Re Agent Orange* Product Liability Litigation, Judgment, District Court of the United States, Eastern District of New York, 28 March 2005, at 136.

[194] *Mazzeo, Julio Lilo and Others*, Judgment, Supreme Court of Argentina, 13 July 2007, para. 15 ('Se trata de la más alta fuente del derecho internacional que se impone a los estados y que prohíbe la comisión de crímenes contra la humanidad, incluso en épocas de guerra' [It is the highest source of international law that is imposed on States and that prohibits the commission of crimes against humanity, even in times of war]). See also *Arancibia Clavel, Enrique Lautaro*, Judgment, Supreme Court of Argentina, 24 August 2004, para. 28, and *Office of the Prosecutor v Priebke*, Judgment, Supreme Court of Argentina, 2 November 1995, paras 2–5.

[195] See, e.g. *Exp No. 0024-2010-PI/TC*, Judgment, Peruvian Constitutional Court, 21 March 2011, para. 53.

Along with torture, the international crimes of piracy, slave-trading, war crimes, crimes against humanity, genocide and apartheid require States, even in the absence of binding international treaty law, to suppress such conduct because 'all States have an interest as they violate values that constitute the foundation of the world public order'.[196]

The list of crimes identified by the South African Court, with the exception of the crime of piracy, corresponds to the Commission's list of the most widely cited examples of norms of *jus cogens* in the articles on State responsibility. Second, the description of these crimes by the Court is similar to the descriptive characteristics provisionally adopted by the Drafting Committee, namely the protection of the 'values that constitute the foundation of the world public order'.[197] Other decisions, such as by the Court of Appeal of Kenya, have also described the prohibition of crimes against humanity in language that confirms its non-derogability.[198]

The *jus cogens* status of the prohibition of war crimes, as a subset of the basic rules of humanitarian law, has also been recognized in decisions of national courts. In *Agent Orange Product Liability Litigation*, the United States District Court held that the 'rules against torture, war crimes and genocide' are *jus cogens*.[199] The Argentine Supreme Court had similarly held that the prohibition of war crimes, including the non-applicability of prescription for war crimes, is *jus cogens*.[200] The Constitutional Court of Colombia also held that rules of humanitarian law 'are binding on States and all parties in

[196] *National Commissioner of Police v Southern African Litigation Centre,* Judgment, South African Constitutional Court, 30 October 2014, para. 137.
[197] Draft conclusion 2, provisionally adopted by the Drafting Committee (see statement of the Chair of the Drafting Committee of 26 July 2017, annex), which refers to the protection of 'fundamental values of the international community'.
[198] See *Attorney-General and Others v Kenya Section of International Commission of Jurists,* Judgment, Court of Appeal of Kenya, 16 February 2018, at 44.
[199] *Legality of the Threat or Use of Nuclear Weapons* (n 111), at p. 257, para. 79 ('It is undoubtedly because a great many rules of humanitarian law applicable in armed conflict are so fundamental to the respect of the human person and 'elementary considerations of humanity' ... that the Hague and Geneva Conventions have enjoyed a broad accession. Further these fundamental rules are to be observed by all States whether or not they have ratified the conventions that contain them, because they constitute intransgressible principles of international customary law'). *In Re Agent Orange Product Liability Litigation.*
[200] *Arancibia Clavel, Enrique Lautaro s/ Homicidio Calificado y Asociación Ilícita y Otros,* Case No. 259, Judgment, Supreme Court of Argentina, 24 August 2004 ('Que esta convención sólo afirma la imprescriptibilidad, lo que importa el reconocimiento de una norma ya vigente (*jus cogens*) en función del derecho internacional público de origen consuetudinario' [That this Convention only affirms imprescriptibility, which is important for the recognition of a norm already in force (*jus cogens*) in function of the public international law of customary origin]).

armed conflict, even if they have not approved the respective treaties, because [of their] peremptoriness'.[201]

5.4   Other Candidates Considered

Beyond the list proposed by the Special Rapporteur, other norms have been cited as norms of *jus cogens* and all enjoy a degree of support. Those most frequently proposed are the prohibition of enforced disappearance, the right to life, the principle of non-refoulement, the prohibition of human trafficking, the right to due process (the right to a fair trial), the prohibition of discrimination, environmental rights, and the prohibition of terrorism. Indeed, there are many norms that have been put forward as candidates for *jus cogens*.[202] As noted in an earlier article on normative hierarchy:

> The literature is replete with claims that particular international norms constitute norms *jus cogens*. Proponents have argued for inclusion of all human rights, all humanitarian norms (human rights and the laws of war), the duty not to cause transboundary environmental harm, the duty to assassinate dictators, the right to life of animals, self-determination, and territorial sovereignty (despite legions of treaties transferring territory from one State to another).

The present section provides a brief account of the support in practice for the peremptory status of some of the norms listed above. This is not a comprehensive review either in breadth or in depth, but serves to indicate the range of other norms that have been proposed for *jus cogens* status. For this purpose, the present section will provide some discussion on three norms that enjoy wide support but are not included in the draft conclusion.

The *jus cogens* nature of the prohibition of enforced disappearance has received a large degree of support in State practice, although it began as a regional norm in the Inter-American System. The main instrument today for the prohibition of enforced disappearance is the United Nations International Convention for the Protection of All Persons from Enforced

---

[201] Judgment No. C-225/95 of the Constitutional Court of Colombia.
[202] See, e.g. D. Shelton, 2014 'International Law and "Relative Normativity"', in M.D. Evans (ed.) *International Law* (4th edn, Oxford, Oxford University Press), ch. 5, pp. 142–172.

Disappearance (hereinafter the 'Enforced Disappearance Convention').[203] Article 1 states, in absolute terms, that '[n]o one shall be subjected to enforced disappearance'.[204] The Enforced Disappearance Convention also provides an indication of the impermissibility of derogations: '[n]o exceptional circumstances whatsoever, whether a state of war or a threat of war, internal political instability or any other public emergency, may be invoked as a justification for enforced disappearance'. It further states that enforced disappearance, when committed as part of a 'widespread or systematic practice', constitutes a crime against humanity (Art. 5).

The recognition of the prohibition of enforced disappearance as a norm of *jus cogens* has been consistent in the Inter-American System. In the case of *Goiburú*, the Inter-American Court of Human Rights held that not only was 'the prohibition of the forced disappearance of persons' a norm of *jus cogens*, but also attributed peremptory status to the 'corresponding obligation to investigate and punish those responsible' for acts of enforced disappearance.[205] In the *Osorio Rivera and Family Members v Peru* case, the Court noted that enforced disappearance 'constitutes a gross violation of human rights' and 'involves a blatant rejection of the essential principles', before affirming that its prohibition was a norm of *jus cogens*.[206]

---

[203] International Convention for the Protection of All Persons from Enforced Disappearance (New York, 20 December 2006), United Nations, *Treaty Series*, vol. 2716, No. 48088, p. 3.

[204] Ibid., Art. 1, para. 2.

[205] *Goiburú* (n 163), para. 84.

[206] *Osorio Rivera and Family Members v Peru*, Judgment (Preliminary objections, merits, reparations, and costs), IACtHR, 26 November 2013, Series C, No. 274, para. 112. See also, for other examples, *García and Family Members v Guatemala*, Judgment (Merits, Reparations and Costs), IACtHR, 29 November 2012, Series C, No. 258, para. 96 ('In sum, the practice of forced disappearance involves a heinous abandonment of the essential principles on which the Inter-American human rights system is founded and its prohibition has achieved *jus cogens* status'); *Gudiel Álvarez et al. (Diario Militar) v Guatemala*, Judgment (Merits, Reparations and Costs), IACtHR, 20 November 2012, Series C, No. 253, para. 232; *Contreras et al. v El Salvador*, Judgment (Merits, Reparations, and Costs), IACtHR, 30 August 2011, Series C, No. 232, para. 83; *Gelman v Uruguay*, Judgment (Merits and Reparations), IACtHR, 24 February 2011, Series C, No. 221, para. 75 ('The practice of enforced disappearance of persons constitutes an inexcusable abandonment of the essential principles on which the Inter-American System of Human Rights is founded, and whose prohibition has reached the character of *jus cogens*'); *Gomes Lund et al. (Guerrilha Do Araguaia) v Brazil*, Judgment (Preliminary Objections, Merits, Reparations, and Costs), IACtHR, 24 November 2010, Series C, No. 219, para. 105; *Ibsen Cárdenas and Ibsen Peña v Bolivia*, Judgment (Merits, Reparations, and Costs), IACtHR, 1 September 2010, Series C, No. 217, paras 61 and 197; *Chitay Nech et al. v Guatemala*, Judgment (Preliminary objections, merits, reparations, and costs), IACtHR, 25 May 2010, Series C, No. 212, para. 193; *Radilla-Pacheco v Mexico*, Judgment (Preliminary objections, merits, reparations, and costs), IACtHR, 23 November 2009, Series C, No. 209, para. 139 ('Forced disappearance constitutes an inexcusable abandonment of the essential principles on which the Inter-American System is based and its prohibition has reached a nature of *jus cogens*'); and

The *jus cogens* character of the prohibition of enforced disappearance has also been recognized in a number of domestic jurisdictions. The
Supreme Court of Argentina stated that the prohibition contained in the
Enforced Disappearance Convention enshrined the non-derogable law of
jus cogens.[207] Similarly, the Constitutional Court of Peru has described the
prohibition of enforced disappearance as part of core non-derogable rules
of peremptory international law, in addition to being part of the Peruvian
constitutional framework.[208] Referring to the Third Restatement, the
United States Court of Appeals has, in *Siderman de Blake*, also referred to
the prohibition of 'causing disappearance of individuals' as a norm of *jus
cogens*.[209]

The right not to be arbitrarily deprived of life is also recognized as non-
derogable in treaty law. Article 6 of the International Covenant on Civil and
Political Rights provides that everyone 'has the inherent right to life' and
further provides that '[n]o one shall be arbitrarily deprived of his life'.[210]
The rights in Article 6 are included in the list of non-derogable rights under
Article 4 of the Covenant. Similarly the European Convention on Human
Rights (ECHR) provides for the right to life and that no one may be deprived of life save in very specifically enumerated circumstances.[211] As with
the International Covenant on Civil and Political Rights, the right to life in
the European Convention is non-derogable.[212] The importance of this right
under the European system has been underscored by the case law, where
the right has been described as 'one of the most fundamental provisions
in the Convention, from which no derogation is permitted' and one which
'enshrines one of the basic values of the democratic societies making up the
Council of Europe'.[213]

The prohibition of arbitrary deprivation of life is also contained in
other human rights instruments, such as the African Charter[214] and the

---

Anzualdo Castro v Peru, Judgment (Preliminary Objections, Merits, Reparations, and Costs),
IACtHR, 22 September 2009, Series C, No. 202, para. 59.

[207] *Simon (Julio Hector) v office of the Public Prosecutor*, Judgment, Supreme Court of
Argentina, 14 June 2005.
[208] *Guillén de Rivero v Peruvian Supreme Court*, Judgment, Constitutional Court of Peru, 12
August 2005.
[209] *Siderman de Blake v Argentina* (n 174), at 714.
[210] ICCPR, Art. 6, para. 1.
[211] European Convention on Human Rights, Art. 2.
[212] Ibid., Art. 15.
[213] *Makaratis v Greece*, No.50385/99, Judgment, Grand Chamber, ECHR 2004-XI (20
December 2004) para. 56.
[214] African Charter on Human and Peoples' Rights, Art. 4.

American Convention on Human Rights.[215] In its general comment No. 29, the Human Rights Committee, while recognizing that not all the rights that were non-derogable under Article 4 were *jus cogens*, expressed the view that the right not be arbitrarily deprived of life was a norm of *jus cogens*.[216] Similarly, the African Commission on Human and Peoples' Rights has stated that the 'right not to be arbitrarily deprived of one's life is recognised as part of customary international law ... and is also recognised as a *jus cogens* norm, universally binding at all times'.[217] The Inter-American Commission has held similarly.[218]

There is also some support for the peremptory character of the right to life, or at least the prohibition on the arbitrary deprivation of life (the right not to be arbitrarily deprived of life). In *Nada v State Secretariat for Economic Affairs,* the Swiss Federal Supreme Court determined that '*jus cogens* includes elementary human rights such as the right to life'.[219] In *RM v Attorney-General,* the High Court of Kenya, having rejected the argument that parental rights were *jus cogens*, said that the closest linkage between the parental rights and *jus cogens* was the right to life (which was *jus cogens*), but did not accept that the actions complained of threatened that right.[220] Finally, the prohibition on arbitrary deprivation of life can be recognized as *jus cogens* despite continued application of the death penalty because, if the death penalty is imposed after strict observance of due process standards and guarantees of a fair trial, it is probably not 'arbitrary'.

[215] American Convention on Human Rights, Art. 4
[216] Human Rights Committee, General Comment No. 29 (2001) on derogations during a state of emergency, ORGA, 56th Sess., supp. No. 40, vol. I, A/56/40, vol. I, annex VI, para. 11.
[217] African Commission HPR, General Comment No. 3 on the African Charter on Human and Peoples' Rights, Art. 4, para. 5.
[218] See *Victims of the Tugboat '13 de Marzo' v Cuba*, Case 11.436, Decision of the IACtHR, 16 October 1996, Report 47/96, para. 79 ('Another point that the Inter-American Commission on Human Rights must stress is that the right to life, understood as a basic right of human beings enshrined in the American Declaration and in various international instruments of regional and universal scope, has the status of *jus cogens*. That is, it is a peremptory rule of international law, and, therefore, cannot be derogable. The concept of *jus cogens* is derived from a higher order of norms established in ancient times and which cannot be contravened by the laws of man or of nations').
[219] *Youssef Nada v State Secretariat for Economic Affairs and Federal Department of Economic Affairs*, Administrative appeal judgment, Case No 1A 45/2007; ILDC 461 (CH 2007); BGE 133 II 450 at 7.3 ('Allgemein werden zum ius cogens elementare menschenrechte wie das Recht auf Leben' [In general, fundamental human rights such as the right to life become *jus cogens*]).
[220] See *RM v Attorney General* (n 178) ('On this, a perusal of the authoritative sources and international jurisprudence reveals that although the applicants are correct in the definition of *jus cogens* as outlined above and its current classifications it has not yet embraced parental responsibility and the rights associated with it. The closest linkage is the right to life and we are not convinced that the challenged section(s) threaten the right to life').

The principle of non-refoulement is another principle of international law whose candidacy for peremptory status has support. In its advisory opinion on *Rights and Guarantees of Children in the Context of Migration and/or in Need of International Protection,* the Inter-American Court of Human Rights linked the principle of non-refoulement to the prohibition of torture and held that because of its relation with the prohibition of torture, the principle 'is absolute and also becomes a peremptory norm of customary international law; in other words, of *ius cogens*'.[221] In response, Latin American States have recognized the jurisprudence of the Court relating to 'the right to seek and be granted asylum enshrined in the regional human rights instruments' and its 'relationship to international refugee instruments [and] the *jus cogens* character of the principle of *non-refoulement*'.[222] The principle has been described by the General Assembly as 'a fundamental principle' which 'is not subject to derogation'.[223] The General Assembly has also '[d]eplore[d] the refoulement and unlawful expulsion of refugees and asylum-seekers'.[224] In 2009, the African Union undertook 'to deploy all necessary measures to ensure full respect for the fundamental principle of non-refoulement'.[225]

There is also much support for the principle in treaty practice. It is contained, in particular, in refugee-related conventions. The Convention relating to the Status of Refugees (hereinafter, 'Refugee Convention') provides for the principle of non-refoulement in its Article 33.[226] Under the Convention, non-refoulement is subject to the security interests of the

---

[221] *Rights and Guarantees of Children in the Context of Migration and/or in Need of International Protection,* Advisory Opinion, IACtHR, 19 August 2014, para. 225.

[222] Brazil Declaration: 'A Framework for Cooperation and Regional Solidarity to Strengthen the International Protection of Refugees, Displaced and Stateless Persons in Latin America and the Caribbean', 3 December 2014.

[223] General Assembly resolution 51/75 of 12 December 1996 on the Office of the UN High Commissioner for Refugees, para. 3. See also General Assembly resolution 34/60 of 29 November 1979 on the report of the UN High Commissioner for Refugees, para. 3, where the General Assembly urged governments to 'grant[] asylum to those seeking refuge and [to] scrupulously observ[e] the principle of *non-refoulement*'.

[224] General Assembly resolution 63/148 of 18 December 2008 on the Office of the UN High Commissioner for Refugees, para. 13.

[225] Kampala Declaration on Refugees, Returnees and Internally Displaced Persons in Africa, 23 October 2009, para. 6.

[226] Convention relating to the Status of Refugees (Geneva, 28 July 1951), UN, *Treaty Series,* vol. 189, No. 2545, p. 137, Art. 33 ('No Contracting State shall expel or return ("refouler") a refugee in any manner whatsoever to the frontiers of territories where his life or freedom would be threatened on account of his race, religion, nationality, membership of a particular social group or political opinion').

State concerned.[227] The Organization of African Unity's Convention Governing the Specific Aspects of Refugee Problems in Africa also contains the principle of non-refoulement with similar exclusions as the Refugee Convention.[228] The Convention against Torture provides for the principle of non-refoulement in the context of torture without any of the restrictions contained in the Refugee Convention.[229] Similarly, the Enforced Disappearance Convention prohibits, in absolute terms, refoulement if it could lead to enforced disappearance.[230]

The present report does not take a view on whether the norms in this section do qualify as norms of *jus cogens*. The Special Rapporteur would note, however, that there is strong support for the *jus cogens* status of these norms. Additionally, there are some other norms whose *jus cogens* status enjoys lesser support. These include the prohibition against arbitrary arrest,[231] the right to due process[232] and others that may in the future be recognized and accepted as non-derogable, including the duty to protect the environment or elements of it and the prohibition of all forms of discrimination.

The principle of non-discrimination is not an easy one. The question has been raised as to why the prohibition of racial discrimination is on most

---

[227] Ibid., Art. 33, para. 2 ('The benefit of the present provision may not, however, be claimed by a refugee whom there are reasonable grounds for regarding as a danger to the security of the country in which he is, or who, having been convicted by a final judgment of a particularly serious crime, constitutes a danger to the community of that country').

[228] OAU Convention Governing Specific Aspects of Refugee Problems in Africa (Addis Ababa, 10 September 1969), United Nations, *Treaty Series*, vol. 1001, No. 14691, p. 45, art. II, para. 3, read with Art. I, para. 5. See also the American Convention on Human Rights, Art. 22, para. 8 ('In no case may an alien be deported or returned to country, regardless of whether or not it is his country of origin, if in that country his right to life or personal freedom is in danger of being violated because of his race, nationality, religion, social status, or political opinion').

[229] Convention against Torture, Art. 3 ('No State Party shall expel, return (*refouler*) or extradite a person to another State where there are substantial grounds for believing that he would be in danger of being subjected to torture').

[230] International Convention for the Protection of All Persons from Enforced Disappearance, Art. 16, para. 1 ('No State Party shall expel, return ('refouler'), surrender or extradite a person to another State where there are substantial grounds for believing that he or she would be in danger of being subjected to enforced disappearance').

[231] *Belhaj v Straw; Rahmatullah v Minister of Defence* (n 182), Opinion of Lord Sumption, para. 271 ('The ... Working Group regarded this irreducible core as *jus cogens*... In my opinion they were right to do so'); *Committee of US Citizens Living in Nicaragua v Reagan* (n 178), 941. See also Report of the Working Group on Arbitrary Detention, United Nations Basic Principles and Guidelines on Remedies and Procedures on the Right of Anyone Deprived of their Liberty to Bring Proceedings Before a Court (A/HRC/30/37), especially at para. 11.

[232] *AA v Austria*, Judgment, Supreme Court of Justice of Austria, 30 September 2008. See, however, *A v State Secretariat for Economic Affairs and Federal Department of Economic Affairs*, Judgment, Switzerland Federal Supreme Court, 22 April 2008, and *Nada v State Secretariat for Economic Affairs* (n 219).

lists but not the prohibition of gender discrimination.[233] There is *some* support for the idea that the prohibition of discrimination *as a whole* is a norm of *jus cogens*. For the most part, the proposition that the prohibition of discrimination as a whole is a peremptory norm can be found in the jurisprudence of the Inter-American Court of Human Rights.[234] From a normative and moral perspective, there can be no argument against this call for the prohibition arbitrary discrimination to be accorded *jus cogens* status. Yet, the Rapporteur finds there is limited explicit *opinio juris*[235] regarding the

---

[233] See generally, H. Charlesworth and C. Chinkin (n 66). In a note to the Fourth Report, the Special Rapporteur indicates his belief that gender discrimination should be prohibited in the same way as other *jus cogens* norms, but signals that one of the hurdles that it has to overcome is the significant number of reservations attached to the Convention on the Elimination of All Forms of Discrimination against Women (New York, 18 December 1979), UN, *Treaty Series*, vol. 1249, No. 20378, p. 13, which has more than 55 reservations. See, Declarations, reservations, objections and notifications of withdrawal of reservations relating to the Convention on the Elimination of All Forms of Discrimination against Women (CEDAW/SP/2006/2). See Fourth Report (n 95), at p. 63.

[234] See, e.g. *Yatama v Nicaragua*, Judgment (Preliminary Objections, Merits, Reparations and Costs), IACtHR, 23 June 2005, Series C, No. 127, para. 184 ('At the current stage of the evolution of international law, the fundamental principle of equality and non-discrimination has entered the realm of *jus cogens*'); *Servellón-García* et al. *v Honduras*, Judgment (Merits, Reparations and Costs), IACtHR, 21 September 2006, Series C, No. 152, para. 94 ('This Tribunal considers that the fundamental principle of equality and non-discrimination belongs to the realm of *jus cogens* that, of a peremptory character, entails obligations *erga omnes* of protection that bind all States and result in effects with regard to third parties, including individuals'); *Expelled Dominicans and Haitians v Dominican Republic*, Judgment (Preliminary Objections, Merits, Reparations, and Costs), IACtHR, 28 August 2014, Series C, No. 282, para. 264 ('the Court reiterates that the *jus cogens* principle of equal and effective protection of the law and non-discrimination requires States, when regulating the mechanisms for granting nationality, to abstain from establishing discriminatory regulations or regulations that have discriminatory effects on different groups of a population when they exercise their rights'); *Norín Catrimán* et al. *(Leaders, Members and Activist of the Mapuche Indigenous People) v Chile*, Judgment (Merits, Reparations and Costs), IACtHR, 29 May 2014, Series C, No. 279, para. 197 ('Regarding the principle of equality before the law and non-discrimination, the Court has indicated that "the notion of equality springs directly from the oneness of the human family, and is linked to the essential dignity of the individual." Thus, any situation is incompatible with this concept that, by considering one group superior to another group, leads to treating it in a privileged way; or, inversely, by considering a given group to be inferior, treats it with hostility or otherwise subjects it to discrimination in the enjoyment of rights that are accorded to those who are not so classified. The Court's case law has also indicated that, at the current stage of the evolution of international law, the fundamental principle of equality and non-discrimination has entered the sphere of *jus cogens*. It constitutes the foundation for the legal framework of national and international public order and permeate[s] the whole legal system.'); *Veliz Franco* et al. *v Guatemala*, Judgment (Preliminary Objections, Merits, Reparations, and Costs), IACtHR, 19 May 2014, Series C, No. 277, para. 205 ('At the actual stage of the evolution of international law, the fundamental principle of equality and non-discrimination has entered the realm of *jus cogens*').

[235] Referring to the acceptance and recognition of the international community of States as a whole. See generally, second report (A/CN.4/706); Fourth Report (n 95), at para.135.

prohibition of discrimination in general or the more limited prohibition of gender discrimination.

By virtue of the importance of the subject matter and the catastrophic consequence that could result from the destruction of the environment,[236] it might seem obvious that norms that aim at protecting the environment should have the status of *jus cogens*.[237] Yet, there seems to be little evidence of the required 'acceptance and recognition of the international community of States as a whole' that the environmental norms have acquired peremptory status, notwithstanding this empirical fact of the importance of environmental rules for the very survival of humanity and the planet.[238] Although not referring to norms of *jus cogens*, John Dugard, in a dissenting opinion, has described particular rules relating to the protection of the environment as establishing obligations *erga omnes*.[239]

The Netherlands Supreme Court judgment in the *Urgenda* case,[240] does not discuss *jus cogens*, but still offers some support for considering the

---

[236] On the importance of the environment, see *Gabčíkovo-Nagymaros Project (Hungary/ Slovakia), Judgment*, ICJ Reports 1997, p. 7, separate opinion of Judge Weeramantry, at pp. 91–92 ('The protection of the environment is likewise a vital part of contemporary human rights doctrine, for it is a *sine qua non* for numerous human rights such as the right to health and the right to life itself. It is scarcely necessary to elaborate on this, as damage to the environment can impair and undermine all the human rights spoken of in the Universal Declaration and other human rights instruments').

[237] This theme was explored in E.M. Kornicker Uhlmann, 1998, 'State community interests, *jus cogens* and protection of the global environment: developing criteria for peremptory norms', 11 *Georgetown Int'l Environmental Law Rev.*, 101–136. Her article was 'based on the premise that today State community interests play a paramount role in the creation of fundamental international norms and that the protection of the global environment is the prototype of a State community interest'.

[238] See, e.g., P. Birnie, A. Boyle, and C. Redgwell, 2009, *International Law and the Environment* (3rd edn, Oxford, Oxford University Press), pp. 109–110 ('No such [*jus cogens*] norms of international environmental law have yet been convincingly identified'). Kornicker Uhlman, in 'State community interests, *jus cogens* and protection of the global environment: developing criteria for peremptory norms', concludes that, while the 'prohibition of willful serious damage to the environment during armed conflicts is a *jus cogens* norm', the 'general prohibition of causing or not preventing environmental damage that threatens the international community as a whole has not yet fully developed into *jus cogens*', ibid., p. 35. See also N.A. Robinson, 'Environmental law: Is an obligation *erga omnes* emerging?', paper presented at a panel discussion at the UN, 4 June 2018. See, however, A. Orakhelashvili, 2006, *Peremptory Norms in International Law* (Oxford, Oxford University Press), p. 65.

[239] *Certain Activities Carried Out by Nicaragua in the Border Area (Costa Rica v Nicaragua)*, Compensation Owed by the Republic of Nicaragua to the Republic of Costa Rica, Judgment, the International Court of Justice, 2 February 2018, dissenting opinion of Judge *ad hoc* Dugard, para. 35 ('The obligation not to engage in wrongful deforestation that results in the release of carbon into the atmosphere and the loss of gas sequestration services is certainly an obligation *erga omnes*').

[240] *Stichting Urgenda v The Netherlands (Ministry of Economic Affairs and Climate Policy)*, Supreme Court of the Netherlands, Judgment of 20 December 2019.

obligation to combat climate change to have peremptory status. In part, the judgment relies on Article 2 of the European Convention on Human Rights and Fundamental Freedoms. This article sets forth a non-derogable right, protecting the right to life. 'According to the case law of the European Court of Human Rights (ECtHR)', cited by the Supreme Court, 'a contracting state is obliged by these provisions to take suitable measures if a real and immediate risk to people's lives or welfare exists and the state is aware of that risk. The obligation to take suitable measures also applies when it comes to environmental hazards that threaten large groups or the population as a whole, even if the hazards will only materialise over the long term'.[241]

In paras 4.2 and 4.7 of the judgment, the Supreme Court summarized the science and facts that underpin its conclusions:

> The emission of greenhouse gases, which are the partial result of burning of fossil fuels and the resultant release of the greenhouse gas CO_2, is leading to an ever-higher concentration of those gases in the atmosphere. This is warming the planet, which is resulting in a variety of hazardous consequences. This may result in local areas of extreme heat, extreme drought, extreme precipitation, or other extreme weather. It is also causing both glacial ice and the ice in and near the polar regions to melt, which is raising the sea level. Some of these consequences are already happening right now. That warming may also result in tipping points, as a result of which the climate on earth or in particular regions of earth changes abruptly and comprehensively. This will result in, among other things, the significant erosion of ecosystems which will, [for] example, jeopardise the food supply, result in the loss of territory and habitable areas, endanger health, and cost human lives.
>
> ....
>
> 4.7 Based on the aforementioned facts, the Court of Appeal concluded, quite understandably, in para. 45 that there was 'a real threat of dangerous climate change, resulting in the serious risk that the current generation of citizens will be confronted with loss of life and/or a disruption of family life'. The Court of Appeal also held, in para. 37, that it was 'clearly plausible that the current generation of Dutch nationals, in particular but not limited to the younger individuals in this group, will have to deal with the adverse effects of climate change in their lifetime if global emissions of greenhouse gases are not adequately reduced.'

---

[241] Ibid., summary.

In its discussion of the law, the Court refers first to the ECHR Article 1, which imposes on States Parties the duty to secure the rights in the Convention to all within the State's jurisdiction. From there it reviews the jurisprudence of the ECHR on the positive obligations of States. According to established ECtHR case law, Article 2 encompasses a contracting State's positive obligation to take appropriate steps to safeguard the lives of those within its jurisdiction.[242] According to that case law, this obligation applies, inter alia, if the situation in question entails hazardous industrial activities, regardless of whether these are conducted by the government itself or by others, and also in situations involving natural disasters. The ECtHR has on multiple occasions found that Article 2 ECHR was violated with regard to a State's acts or omissions in relation to a natural or environmental disaster.[243] Again, although the Supreme Court does not heavily rely on the non-derogable status of the right to life, that element is implicit in the judgement.

It may well be that some rules, like those relating to the environment, will be found to have the status of *jus cogens* although have yet to be accepted and recognized by the international community of States as a whole.[244] Yet, as this discussion has shown, the number and diversity of norms that have been put forward as candidates for *jus cogens* are ever growing.

---

[242] See, inter alia, ECtHR 28 March 2000, No. 22492/93 (Kiliç/Turkey), para. 62, and ECtHR 17 July 2014, No. 47848/08 (Centre for Legal Resources on behalf of Valentin Câmpeanu/ Romania), para. 130.

[243] Cf., inter alia, the following judgments in which the ECtHR held that the requirements set out here were met: ECtHR 30 November 2004, No. 48939/99 (Öneryildiz/Turkey), paras 98–101 (gas explosion at landfill; the risk of this occurring at any time had existed for years and had been known to the authorities for years); ECtHR 20 March 2008, No. 15339/02 (Budayeva et al./Russia), paras 147–158 (life-threatening mudslide; the authorities were aware of the danger of mudslides there and of the possibility that they might occur at some point on the scale it actually did); and ECtHR 28 February 2012, No. 17423/05 (Kolyadenko et al./Russia), paras 165 and 174–180 (necessary outflow from the reservoir because of exceptionally heavy rains; the authorities knew that in the event of exceptionally heavy rains evacuation might be necessary). See in this sense also Administrative Jurisdiction Division of the Council of State 18 November 2015, ECLI:NL:RVS:2015:3578 (Gas extraction in Groningen), para. 39.3.

[244] See, for discussion, first report (A/CN.4/693), para. 59. See also M. Koskenniemi, 2006, *From Apology to Utopia: The Structure of Legal Argument* (Cambridge, Cambridge University Press), pp. 307 ff., especially p. 308 ('neither contrasting position can be consistently preferred because they also rely on each other'). At p. 323, specifically on *jus cogens*, he says: 'Initially, *jus cogens* seems to be descending, non-consensualist. It seems to bind States irrespective of their consent. But a law which would make no reference to what States have consented to would seem to collapse into a natural morality [but] the reference to recognition by "international community of States" [makes it] ... ascending, consensualist'.

6

Jus Cogens in Recent Legal Scholarship*

Writers continue to discuss and debate the origins and sources of *jus cogens*.[1] In addition, they devote increasing attention to the specific norms proposed for such status. The prohibition of enforced disappearance, for example, has been recognized in writings as a norm of *jus cogens*. Criddle and Fox-Decent, whose fiduciary theory of *jus cogens* serves to prevent 'flagrant abuses of State power [that] deny a State's beneficiaries secure and equal freedom', would include as a norm of *jus cogens* the prohibition of 'forced disappearances'.[2] The prohibition of torture is also accepted as *jus*

---

* This chapter draws upon materials published in: Dinah Shelton, 'Sherlock Holmes and the mystery of jus cogens', 46 Netherlands Yearbook of International Law, (2015) 23–50. Reprinted with permission. Dinah Shelton, 'International Law and "Relative Normativity"' in M.D Evans (ed.), International Law, (4th edn, OUP 2014) 137–166.

[1] See, e.g. R. Ago, 1971, 'Droit des traités à la lumière de la Convention de Vienne', *134 Collected Courses of The Hague Academy of Int Law*, 324; C. Mik, 2013, '*Jus cogens* in contemporary international law', *33 Polish Yearb. Int'l Law*, 27–93, at 59; S. Kadelbach, 2015, 'Genesis, function and identification of *jus cogens* norms', *46 Netherlands Yearb. Int'l Law*, 147–172, at 151; A. Bianchi, 2008,'Human rights and the magic of *jus cogens*', *19 Eur. J. Int'l Law*, 491–508, at 495; E.J. Criddle and E. Fox-Decent, 2009, 'A fiduciary theory of *jus cogens*', *34 Yale J. Int'l Law*, 331–387, at 355; S. Knuchel, 2015, Jus cogens: *Identification and Enforcement of Peremptory Norms* (Zurich, Schulthess), p. 41; D. Costelloe, 2017, *Legal Consequences of Peremptory Norms in International Law* (Cambridge, Cambridge University Press), p. 16; A. Cassese, 2012, 'For an enhanced role of *jus cogens*', in A. Cassese (ed.) *Realizing Utopia: The Future of International Law* (Oxford, Oxford University Press), p. 162; M.C. Bassiouni, 1996, 'International crimes: *jus cogens* and obligations erga omnes', *59 Law and Contemporary Problems*, 63–74, at 70; and T. Cottier, 2015, 'Improving compliance: *jus cogens* and international economic law', *46 Netherlands Yearb. Int'l Law*, 329–356, at 133; A.A. Cançado Trindade, 2008, '*Jus cogens*: The determination and the gradual expansion of its material content in contemporary international case-law', *35 Curso de Derecho Internacional (Organization of American States, Inter-American Juridical Committee)*, 3–30, at 13; M. den Heijer and H. van der Wilt, 2015, '*Jus cogens* and the humanization and fragmentation of international law', *46 Netherlands Yearb. Int'l Law*, 3–21, at 9; J.E. Christófolo, 2016, *Solving Antinomies between Peremptory Norms in Public International Law* (Geneva, Schulthess), p. 219.

[2] Criddle and Fox-Decent (n 1) at 369–370. See also J. Sarkin, 2012, 'Why the prohibition of enforced disappearance has attained *jus cogens* status in international law', *81 Nordic J. Int'l Law*, 537–583; A.A. Cançado Trindade, 2012, 'Enforced disappearances of persons as a violation of *jus cogens*: The contribution of the Inter-American Court of Human Rights', *81 Nordic J. Int'l Law*, 507–536; D. Shelton, 2015, 'Sherlock Holmes and the mystery of *jus cogens*', *46 Neth. Yearb Int'l Law*, 23–50, at 39; and Kadelbach (n 1) at 168.

cogens in the literature.[3] Tomuschat, for example, states that 'offences which debase the affected individual, striking at his/her dignity and existence, must be comprised in the circle of norms coming with the purview of *jus cogens*', including the 'prohibition[] on ... torture'.[4]

Several writers have described the principle of non-refoulement as a norm of *jus cogens*. These include Allain, Orakhelashvili, and Farmer.[5] There have, of course, been authors who have concluded that the principle of non-refoulement is not a norm of *jus cogens*.[6] Cassese regarded the principle of non-refoulement as an emerging norm of *jus cogens*.[7] Costello and Foster offer an in-depth analysis, looking at both arguments for and against, and come to the conclusion that the principle of non-refoulement is a norm of *jus cogens*.[8]

Unsurprisingly, there is also ample support in academic writings for the view that the prohibition of crimes against humanity is a norm of *jus cogens*.[9] Where lists of norms of *jus cogens* are provided, invariably the prohibition of crimes against humanity is included.[10] Even when not identifying the

---

[3] See generally, E. de Wet, 2004, 'The prohibition of torture as an international norm of *jus cogens* and its implications for national and customary law', *15 Eur. J. Int'l Law*, 97–121. See also E. de Wet, 2006, 'The emergence of international and regional value systems as a manifestation of the emerging international constitutional order', *19 Leiden J. Int'l Law* 611–632, at 616.

[4] C. Tomuschat, 2015, 'The Security Council and *jus cogens*', in E. Cannizzaro (ed.) *The Present and Future of Jus Cogens* (Rome, Sapienza), p. 36. See also A. Pellet, 2006, 'Comments in response to Christine Chinkin and in defense of *jus cogens* as the best bastion against the excesses of fragmentation', *17 Finnish Yearb. Int'l Law*, 83–89, at 83; K. Parker and L.B. Neylon, 1988–1989, '*Jus cogens*: Compelling the law of human rights', *11 Hastings Int'l and Comparative Law Rev.*, 411–464, at 414; Cançado Trindade (n 1) at 5.

[5] See J. Allain, 2001, 'The *jus cogens* nature of non-refoulement', *13 Int'l J. Refugee Law*, 533–558; A. Farmer, 2008, 'Non-refoulement and *jus cogens*: Limiting anti-terror measures that threaten refugee protection', *23 Georgetown Immigration Law J.*, 1–38; and A. Orakhelashvili, 2006, *Peremptory Norms of General International Law* (Oxford, Oxford University Press), p. 56.

[6] See e.g., A. Duffy, 2008, 'Expulsion to face torture? *Non-refoulement* in international law', *20 International Journal of Refugee Law*, 373–390, who expresses doubt about the *jus cogens* status of non-refoulement.

[7] Cassese (n 1) at pp. 162–163.

[8] C. Costello and M. Foster, 2015, 'Non-refoulement as custom and *jus cogens*? Putting the prohibition to the test', *46 Netherlands Yearb. Int'l Law*, 273–323; and Allain (n 5). For a discussion of the implication of this, see Farmer (n 5). See however, *Sale v Haitian Centers Council*, Judgment, US Supreme Court, 21 June 1993, which upheld an executive order permitting refoulment. See, for discussion, H.H. Koh, 1994, 'Reflections on *refoulement* and the Haitian Centers Council', *35 Harvard Int'l Law J.*, 1–20.

[9] See, e.g. den Heijer and van der Wilt (n 1) at 9.

[10] See, e.g. U. Linderfalk, 2015, 'Understanding the jus cogens debate: The pervasive influence of legal positivism and legal idealism', *46 Netherlands Yearb. Int'l Law*, 51–84, at 53; T. Kleinlein, 2015, 'Jus cogens as the "highest law"? Peremptory norms and legal hierarchies', *46 Netherlands Yearb. Int'l Law*, 110–197, at 197; L.J. Kotzé, 2015, 'Constitutional conversations in the Anthropocene: In search of environmental *jus cogens* norms', *46 Netherlands Yearb. Int'l Law*, 241–272, at 243; Criddle and Fox-Decent (n 1) at 369; and E. de Wet, 2013, '*Jus cogens*

prohibition of crimes against humanity explicitly as *jus cogens*, authors tend to assume its peremptory status.[11] Leila Sadat, for example, without explicitly stating that the prohibition of crimes against humanity is *jus cogens*, observes that the provisions in the Commission's draft articles on crimes against humanity are appropriate for 'a convention addressing a *jus cogens* offence with the robust inter-State cooperation, mutual legal assistance and enforcement provisions'.[12] In this respect, Christófolo observes that the 'peremptory nature of the prohibition of crimes against humanity is inscribed within the same normative development of other norms of *ius cogens*'.[13]

Various publications have also generally recognized the prohibition of apartheid and racial discrimination as a norm of *jus cogens*.[14] The clear recognition of the prohibition of apartheid and racial discrimination as a norm of *jus cogens* is aptly captured by Pellet, who states that 'the universal (official) reprobation of racial discrimination has certainly resulted in a "peremptorization" of the prohibition of racial discrimination (at least when committed on a large and/or systematic scale)'.[15]

The prohibition of slavery is also recognized in academic writings as a norm of *jus cogens*.[16] The *jus cogens* status of the prohibition of slavery is so well accepted that Trindade has remarked, 'I understand that no one … would dare to deny that, e.g. slave work … would likewise affront the universal juridical conscience, and effectively collide with the peremptory norms of the *jus cogens*'.[17] Similarly, den Heijer and van der Wilt

---

and obligations *erga omnes*', in D. Shelton (ed.) *The Oxford Handbook of International Human Rights Law* (Oxford, Oxford University Press), pp. 541–561.

[11]   See, e.g. Shelton (n 2) at 37 where she gives the invocation of accountability for crimes against humanity as an example of a function of *jus cogens* beyond rendering treaties void.

[12]   L.N. Sadat, 2018, 'A contextual and historical analysis of the International Law Commission's 2017 draft articles for a new global treaty on crimes against humanity', *16 J. Int'l Criminal Justice*, 683–704, at 688, 700 ('This language should be stronger still in light of current State and international practice, and given the *jus cogens* nature of crimes against humanity').

[13]   Christófolo (n 1) at p. 219.

[14]   See J. Dugard, 2018, *Confronting Apartheid: A Personal History of South Africa, Namibia and Palestine* (Johannesburg, Jacana), pp. 86, 137. See also Ago (n 1) at 324; Costelloe (n 1) at p. 16; Christófolo (n 1) at p. 222; Knuchel (n 1) at p. 41; de Wet 2006 (n 3) at 616; Cassese (n 1) at p. 162; and Cottier (n 1).

[15]   Pellet (n 4) at 85.

[16]   See, e.g., Ago (n 1) at 324, fn 37. See also A. Verdross, 1966, '*Jus dispositivum* and *jus cogens* in international law', *60 Am. J. Int'l Law* 55–63, at 59; Mik (n 1) at 59; Kadelbach (n 1) at 151; Bianchi (n 1) at 495; Criddle and Fox-Decent (n 1) at 355; Knuchel (n 1) at p. 41; Costelloe (n 1) at p. 16; Cassese (n 1) at p. 162; Bassiouni (n 1) at 70; and Cottier (n 1) at 133.

[17]   Cançado Trindade (n 1) at 13.

include slavery among *jus cogens* norms 'beyond contestation'.[18] Likewise, Christófolo states that 'it seems undisputable that the general prohibition of slavery and slave trade has reached a universal peremptory nature in public international law'.[19]

Writers have generally recognized the right of self-determination as a peremptory norm.[20] whose *jus cogens* status is 'widely undisputed'.[21] Alexidze, similarly, expresses the view that the *jus cogens* status of the right to self-determination is beyond dispute.[22] He states, definitively, that there is 'not a single corner on the Earth' that would not recognize the fundamental importance of self-determination.[23] '[E]qual rights and self-determination of peoples', he asserts, are among the 'principles any derogation from which is *absolutely* forbidden, even *inter se*'.[24] He includes the right to self-determination as one of those norms whose *jus cogens* status is 'obvious'.[25] Mik notes that norms that are principles should not be accorded *jus cogens* status.[26] This would include a rule like the right to self-determination. However, he notes that a principle such as the right to self-determination may have regulatory implications and can thus may not be recognized as a norm of *jus cogens*.[27]

The *jus cogens* status of basic rules of humanitarian law is also generally recognized in the literature.[28] Kleinlein, having identified those norms that the International Court of Justice has described as *jus cogens* (torture and

---

[18] den Heijer and van der Wilt (n 1) at 9.

[19] Christófolo (n 1) at p. 219.

[20] See, e.g., S.Y. Marochkin, 2009, 'On the recent development of international law: Some Russian perspectives', 8 *Chinese J. Int'l Law*, 695–714, at 710; Tomuschat (n 4) at p. 35; J.A. Frowein, 2009, 'Jus *cogens* and obligations erga omnes', in R. Wolfrum (ed.) *Max Planck Encyclopaedia of Public International Law* (Oxford, Oxford University Press), vol. *VI*, p. 444, para. 8.

[21] Kadelbach (n 1) at 152; E. Santalla Vargas, 'In quest of the practical value of jus cogens norms', 46 *Netherlands Yearb. Int'l Law*, 211–239, at 227. See also Pellet (n 4) at 86.

[22] L. Alexidze, 1981, 'The legal nature of *jus cogens* in contemporary international law', *Collected Courses of the Hague Academy of International Law* (The Hague Academy), vol. 172, pp. 219–270, at p. 229..

[23] Ibid., at p. 251.

[24] Ibid., at p. 260. He notes further that the principle of territorial integrity, while also fundamental, can be derogated from as long as the principle of self-determination is observed.

[25] Ibid., at p. 262.

[26] Mik (n 1) at 34.

[27] Ibid. See also at 36, 82, and 83 for confirmation of the peremptory status of *jus cogens*.

[28] See Christófolo (n 1); den Heijer and van der Wilt (n 1) at 12; Linderfalk (n 10) at 53; A. Orakhelashvili, 2015, 'Audience and authority: The merit of the doctrine of *jus cogens*', 46 *Netherlands Yearb. Int'l Law*, 115–146, at 138 ff; Kleinlein (n 10) at 184; Knuchel (n 1) at p. 41; Bassiouni (n 1) at 70; and Frowein (n 20) at p. 443, para. 3.

genocide), states that the '[m]ore inclusive lists also refer to war crimes and the basic principles of international humanitarian law'.[29]

In respect to other issues, Mark Hanna addresses the substantive/procedural distinction as discussed in international and domestic case law.[30] He notes the tension between doctrines of sovereignty and independence that underlie the recognition of sovereign immunity and the expectation of a global public order that have led to an expanding invocation of *jus cogens*. This 'hard case of contemporary international law' as he describes it, has given rise to the 'subtle yet profoundly significant' solution of applying judicially created distinctions, in these matters, a constructed distinction between substantive *jus cogens* norms and the procedural rule of sovereign immunity.

Many authors have criticized this judicial approach[31] while others defend it.[32] Tomuschat, for example, holds that the distinction makes for 'orderly' proceedings, 'protecting the interests of all victims by ensuring equality and non-discrimination'.[33] Hanna takes a different view, which strives to analyse the distinction between substance and procedure in the light of 'the normative expectations of an increasingly globalized society' in which international law 'has evolved into an expansive and complex legal system'.[34] He uses systems analysis to posit the utility of the distinction in maintaining international law's functional relevance in a globalized society with its 'conflicting structure of state sovereignty and global public order'.[35]

---

[29] Kleinlein (n 10) at 197.

[30] M. Hanna, 2018, 'The substantive/procedural distinction: Law's solution to the problem of *Jus Cogens* in a world of sovereign states', *19 German Law J.*, 21–42, at 21.

[31] See, e.g. L. McGregor, 2007, 'Torture and state immunity: Deflecting impunity, distorting sovereignty', *18 Eur.J. Int'l Law*, 903–919, at 911; P.D. Ciaccio, 2008, 'A torturer's manifesto? impunity through immunity in *Jones v The Kingdom of Saudi Arabia*', *30 Sydney Law Rev.*, 551–564, at 557; J. Besner and A. Attaran, 2008, 'Civil liability in Canada's courts for torture committed abroad: The unsatisfactory interpretation of the State Immunity Act of 1985', *16 Tort Law Rev.*, 150–167, at 164.

[32] See S. Talmon, 2012, '*Jus Cogens* after *Germany v Italy* Substantive and procedural rules distinguished', *25 Leiden J. Int'l Law*, 979–1002, at 986.

[33] C. Tomuschat, 2014, 'The case of *Germany v Italy* before the ICJ', in Anne Peters et al. (eds) *Immunities in the Age of Global Constitutionalism* (The Hague, Martinus Nijhoff), p. 88.

[34] Hanna (n 30) at 24.

[35] Ibid., at 25.

7
Functions of *Jus Cogens**

The asserted functions of *jus cogens* are particularly important because the very definition of the term is often stated in relation to the primary function it serves, that is, on its being a norm from which no states can derogate by mutual agreement. A second function is sometimes asserted: that *jus cogens* imposes a duty on all states to respect such norms and as a consequence any unilateral act in violation of a *jus cogens* norm would be null and void. There is little state practice or jurisprudence in respect to either function; the actual function appears to be more expressive, being an important, though symbolic declaration of societal values. These are each discussed in turn in this final chapter.

7.1 The Law of Treaties

Alfred von Verdross's influential 1937 article, 'Forbidden Treaties in International Law', written in the shadow of Nazi Germany, argued that certain rules of international custom have a compulsory character notwithstanding contrary state agreements. Courts must set aside such agreements when they conflict with the 'ethical minimum recognized by all the states of the international community',[1] including the imperative 'moral tasks' of states to maintain law and order, defend against external attacks and ensure the welfare of their citizens.[2] Illegal treaties would thus include those 'binding a state to reduce its police or its organization of courts in such a way that it is no longer able to protect at all or in an adequate manner, the life, the liberty, the honor, or the property of men on its territory'.[3] Treaties might also violate *jus cogens* if they oblige 'a state to close its hospitals or

* This chapter draws upon materials published in: Dinah Shelton, 'Sherlock Holmes and the mystery of jus cogens', 46 Netherlands Yearbook of International Law, (2015) 23–50. Reprinted with permission.
[1] A. von Verdross, 1937, 'Forbidden treaties in international law: Comments on Professor Garner's report on "The Law of Treaties"', *31 Am. J. Int'l Law* 571, 574.
[2] Ibid.
[3] Ibid.

schools, to extradite or sterilize its women, to kill its children, to close its factories, to leave its fields unploughed, or in other ways to expose its population to distress'.[4] Taking up the issue in its work on the law of treaties, the ILC included draft articles on *jus cogens*, which were retained with some amendments as Articles 53 and 64 of the 1969 Vienna Convention on the Law of Treaties. Outside the area of nullity of agreements or provisions therein, the Commission's Guide to Practice on Reservations to Treaties provides analysis on the effects of *jus cogens* on the permissibility and consequences of reservations.[5]

In addition to questions about the hierarchy of norms and the effects of peremptory norms, much recent debate has also centred on whether or not State behaviour in adopting and complying with non-binding instruments evidences acceptance of new modes of lawmaking not reflected in the Statute of the International Court of Justice. Of course, efforts to resolve social problems are not invariably in the form of law in any community. Societies strive to maintain order, prevent and resolve conflicts, and assure justice in the distribution and use of resources not only through law, but through other means of action. Issues of justice may be addressed through market mechanisms and private charity, while conflict resolution can be promoted through education and information, as well as negotiations outside legal institutions. Maintenance of order and societal values can occur through moral sanctions, exclusions, and granting or withholding of benefits, as well as by use of legal penalties and incentives. In the international arena, just as at other levels of governance, law is one form of social control or normative claim, but basic requirements of behaviour also emerge from morality, courtesy, and social custom, reflecting the values of society. They form part of the expectations of social discourse, and compliance with such norms may be expected and violations sanctioned.

Legal regulation, however, has become perhaps the most prevalent response to social problems during the last century. Laws reflect the current needs and recognize the present values of society. Law is often deemed a

---

[4] Ibid., at 575.

[5] See, e.g. commentary to draft guides 3.1.5.4 and 4.4.3. International Law Commission, Guide to practice on reservations to treaties with commentaries, 63rd session of the ILC, UN Doc. A/66/10/Add.1, 2011. See also *Armed Activities on the Territory of the Congo (New Application 2002: Democratic Republic of the Congo v Rwanda)*, ICJ, Judgment of 3 February 2006, Separate Opinion of Judge Dugard, para. 9 (discussing the effect of reservations that violate *jus cogens*); Principle 8 of the International Law Commission, Guiding principles applicable to unilateral declarations of states capable of creating legal obligations, with commentaries thereto, 58th sess. of the ILC, UN Doc. A/61/10, 2006, Principle 8.

necessary, if usually insufficient, basis for ordering behaviour. The language of law, especially written language, most precisely communicates expectations and produces reliance, despite inevitable ambiguities and gaps. It exercises a pull towards compliance by its very nature. Its enhanced value and the more serious consequences of non-conformity lead to the generally accepted notion that fundamental fairness requires some identification of what is meant by 'law', some degree of transparency and understanding of the authoritative means of creating binding norms and the relative importance among them. A law perceived as legitimate and fair is more likely to be observed. This alone makes the issue of relative normativity an important topic, but recent evolution in the international legal system has fostered a burgeoning interest in the issue.

The first development centres on the role of consent in determining legal obligation. International law has traditionally been defined as a system of equal and sovereign States whose actions are limited only by rules freely accepted as legally binding.[6] The emergence of global resource crises such as the widespread depletion of commercial fish stocks, destruction of the stratospheric ozone layer, and anthropogenic climate change, has produced growing concern about the 'free rider', the holdout State that benefits from legal regulation accepted by others while enhancing its own profits through continued utilization of the resource or by ongoing production and sale of banned substances. The traditional consent-based international legal regime lacks a legislature to override the will of dissenting States,[7] but efforts to affect their behaviour are being made; first, through the doctrine of peremptory norms applicable to all States, and second, through expanding the concept of international law to include 'soft law'. The same approach may be taken with States seeking to denounce or acting to violate multilateral agreements that reflect widely and deeply held values, such as human rights or humanitarian law.

The second development that spurs consideration of relative normativity is the substantial expansion of international law. Until the twentieth century, treaties were nearly all bilateral and the subject matter of international legal regulation mostly concerned diplomatic relations, the seas and other international waterways, trade, and extradition. Today, the number of

---

[6] See *Lotus*, Judgment No. 9, 1927, PCIJ, Ser. A, No. 10, at p. 18.
[7] Thus Salcedo argues that 'In principle ... most rules of international law are only authoritative for those subjects that have accepted them' (J.A.C. Salcedo, 1997, 'Reflections on the hierarchy of norms in international law', *8 Eur. J. Int'l Law* 583, 584).

international instruments has grown substantially, multilateral regulatory treaties are common, the topics governed by international law have proliferated, and non-State actors are increasingly part of the system. This complexity demands consideration and development of means to reconcile conflicts of norms within a treaty or given subject area, for example, law of the sea, as well as across competing regimes, such as free trade and environmental protection.

Third, the emergence of international criminal law has led to considering the nature of international crimes and the relationship of this body of law to doctrines of obligations *jus cogens*, discussed below, and obligations *erga omnes*. The ICJ was the first to identify the category of obligations *erga omnes* in *dicta* in the *Barcelona Traction* case.[8] Unlike obligations arising in respect to specific injured States (for example, in the field of diplomatic protection), obligations *erga omnes* are owed to the international community as a whole. The broad nature of the obligation could be based upon the fact that such obligations generally aim at regulating the internal behaviour of a State, such as in the field of human rights, and thus there are likely to be no States materially affected by a breach. The principle of effectiveness thus supports broad standing, because without it violations could not be challenged. However, the rationale stated by the ICJ for recognizing this category of obligations appears more substantive: that 'in view of the importance of the rights involved, all States can be held to have a legal interest in their protection'.[9] This statement suggests that obligations *erga omnes* have specific and broad procedural consequences *because of* the substantive importance of the norms they enunciate. In addition, the fact that all States can complain of a breach may make it more likely that a complaint will be made following commission of a wrongful act, suggesting a higher priority accorded these norms even if they are not considered substantively superior. The ICJ's examples of such obligations included the outlawing of aggression and genocide and the protection from slavery and racial discrimination. Nonetheless, the ILC has concluded that obligations *erga omnes* do not implicate normative hierarchy; while all *jus cogens*

---

[8] *Barcelona Traction*, Light and Power Company, Ltd, Second Phase, Judgment, ICJ Reports 1970, p. 3, para. 33.

[9] Ibid. See also East Timor (*Portugal v Australia*), Judgment, ICJ Reports 1995, p. 90, para. 29; Application of the Convention on the Prevention and Punishment of the Crime of Genocide, Preliminary Objections, Judgment, ICJ Reports 1996, p. 595, para. 31.

obligations have an *erga omnes* character, the reverse is not necessarily true.[10]

Like obligations *erga omnes*, international crimes are so designated because the acts they sanction are deemed of such importance to the international community that individual criminal responsibility should result from their commission.[11] Unlike obligations *erga omnes*, however, international criminal norms can pose problems of relative normativity. First, the question has been posed as to whether there is a hierarchy among the crimes. Second, it has been clear since the Nuremberg Trials that conforming to or carrying out domestic law is no excuse for a breach of international criminal law; it would seem plausible as well, if unlikely to arise in practice, that a defence would fail based on carrying out norms of international law, such as those contained in a bilateral treaty, if those norms contradict the requirements of criminal law.[12] In this respect, norms of criminal law could be given supremacy over other international law in practice.

Other aspects of the inter-relationship of these categories of norms and the sources that create them should be noted. First, neither the designation of international crimes or obligations *erga omnes* involves a purported new source of law; crimes are created and defined through the conclusion of treaties; obligations *erga omnes* through treaty and customary international law. Secondly, it appears logical that all international crimes are obligations *erga omnes* because the international community as a whole identifies and may prosecute and punish the commission of such crimes. The reverse is not the case, however. Not all obligations *erga omnes* have been designated as international crimes. Non-systemic racial discrimination, for example, is cited as an obligation *erga omnes*, but is largely excluded from international crimes.

Among those acts designated as international crimes, there appears to be no hierarchy. The ICTY has rejected the notion of hierarchy, declaring in

---

[10] International Law Commission, Report of the Study Group on Fragmentation of International Law: Difficulties arising from the Diversification and Expansion of International Law, A/CN.4/l.676, 29 July 2005, paras 48 and 50.

[11] The collective nature of the State as subject of international law makes imposition of State criminal responsibility problematic. Although the ILC included a provision on State crimes in early versions of its articles on State responsibility, the provision was eventually excluded.

[12] The treaty itself might be considered void as a violation of peremptory norms if it required or authorized the commission of an international crime.

the *Tadić* judgment that 'there is in law no distinction between the seriousness of a crime against humanity and that of a war crime'.[13]

AS discussed earlier, the extent to which the international legal system has
moved and may still move towards the imposition of global public policy on
non-consenting States remains highly debated, but the need for limits on
State freedom of action seems to be increasingly recognized. International
legal instruments and doctrine now often refer to the 'common interest of
humanity'[14] or 'common concern of mankind' to identify broad concerns
that could form part of international public policy. References are also
more frequent to 'the international community' as an entity or authority
of collective action.[15] In addition, multilateral international agreements increasingly contain provisions that affect non-party States, either providing
incentives to adhere to the norms, or allowing parties to take coercive measures that in practice require conforming behaviour of States not adhering to
the treaty. The UN Charter itself contains a list of fundamental principles
and in Article 2(6) asserts that these may be imposed on non-parties if necessary to ensure international peace and security.

In practice, the concept has been invoked largely outside its original
context in the law of treaties. At the International Court of Justice the
term first appeared only in separate or dissenting opinions;[16] States still
rarely raised the issue[17] and until recently the Court seemed to take pains
to avoid any pronouncement on it.[18] In 2006, however, in its *Congo v
Rwanda* judgment,[19] the Court affirmed both the existence of peremptory
norms in international law, and asserted that the prohibition of genocide
is 'assuredly' such a norm. Nonetheless, the Court emphasized that the *jus*

---

[13] *Prosecutor v Duško Tadić*, Case No. IT-94-1-A, Judgment in Sentencing Appeals, Appeals
Chamber (26 January 2000), para. 69. For a criticism of this view and discussion of the conflicting practice of the ICTY.
[14] See, UNCLOS, Art. 137(2); Treaty on Principles Governing the Activities of States in the
Exploration and Use of Outer Space, Including the Moon and Other Celestial Bodies (1967),
pmbl., para. 2.
[15] See, e.g. Art. 53, VCLT; Arts 136–137 UNCLOS.
[16] See, e.g. Right of Passage over Indian Territory, Merits, Judgment, ICJ Reports 1960, p. 6
at pp. 135 and 139–140 (Judge ad hoc Renandes dissenting); South West Africa, Second Phase,
Judgment, ICJ Reports 1966, p. 6 at p. 298 (Judge Tanaka dissenting).
[17] *Gabcíkovo-Nagymaros Project (Hungary/Slovakia)*, Judgment, ICJ Reports 1997, p. 7,
para. 112, noting that neither side had contended that new peremptory norms of environmental law had emerged.
[18] See *North Sea Continental Shelf*, Judgment, ICJ Reports 1969, p. 3, para. 72, declining to
enter into or pronounce upon any issue concerning *jus cogens*.
[19] Armed Activities on the Territory of the Congo (New Application 2002) (*Congo v
Rwanda*), Judgment of 3 February 2006, para. 64.

cogens status of the prohibition of genocide did not have an impact on its jurisdiction, which remained governed by consent. A dissenting opinion questioned whether the *jus cogens* prohibition of genocide meant that a reservation to the Court's jurisdiction might be incompatible with the object and purpose of the Genocide Convention, but the 'novelty and far-reaching implications' of declaring that *jus cogens* trumps reservations restrained other judges. A year later, the ICJ restated its recognition of *jus cogens* in the *Genocide* case.

Neither *jus cogens* nor peremptory norms have been mentioned in decisions of the UN Tribunal for the Law of the Sea, nor have they been referred to by the Iran or Iraq Claims Tribunals. Human rights tribunals until quite recently also avoided pronouncing on *jus cogens*. In its first human rights judgment to discuss *jus cogens*, decided in 2002, a Grand Chamber of the European Court of Human Rights, by a 9:8 majority, denied that violation of the peremptory norm against torture could act to deprive a State of sovereign immunity.[20] The Court agreed that torture is a peremptory norm, a fundamental value and an absolute right, but found that it was 'unable to discern' any basis for overriding State immunity from civil suit where acts of torture are alleged.

In the Inter-American Court of Human Rights, the term has been increasingly referred to since its first mention in the 2003 advisory opinion on the juridical condition and rights of undocumented migrants.[21] Mexico requested the opinion largely to indicate its concern with domestic labour laws and practices in the United States. Perhaps in an effort to anticipate possible US arguments that it has not consented to relevant international norms, Mexico's fourth question to the Court asked: 'What is the nature today of the principle of non-discrimination and the right to equal and effective protection of the law in the hierarchy of norms established by general international law and, in this context, can they be considered to be the expression of norms *jus cogens*?' Mexico also asked the Court to indicate the legal effect of a finding that these norms are *jus cogens*. Written interventions of the Inter-American Commission, and two briefs from university

---

[20] *Al-Adsani v United Kingdom*, Judgment, 21 November 2001, (2002) 34 EHRR 11. See also *Fogarty v UK* and *McElhinney v Ireland*, decided the same day as *Al-Adsani*. For a critique of the case, see A. Clapham, 2007, 'The *Jus Cogens* Prohibition of Torture and the Importance of Sovereign State Immunity', in M.G. Kohen (ed.) *Promoting Justice, Human Rights and Conflict Resolution through International Law: Liber Amicorum Lucius Caflisch* (The Hague, Martinus Nijhoff), pp. 151–170.

[21] Juridical Condition and Rights of the Undocumented Migrants, Advisory Opinion, OC-18/03 Ser. A, No. 18 (17 September 2003).

amici curiae commented on the topic of *jus cogens*. Costa Rica expressly disavowed any intention to comment on the topic. Mexico asserted that unnamed publicists have denominated fundamental human rights as norms *jus cogens*. It also referred to the views of individual judges and the International Law Commission on the legal effects of *jus cogens*. The main argument of Mexico, however, was that 'international morality', as a source of law, provides a basis for establishing norms *jus cogens*, arguing for the 'transfer' of the Martens clause from humanitarian law to the field of human rights to imply new norms and obligations, even those characterized as *jus cogens*.

The Commission's position simply asserted that the international community is unanimous in considering the prohibition of racial discrimination as an obligation *erga omnes*, then leaps to the conclusion that the principle of non-discrimination is a norm *jus cogens*, while at the same time noting that the international community has not yet reached consensus on prohibiting discrimination based on motives other than racial discrimination. According to the Commission 'this does not lessen its fundamental importance in all international laws'.

The Court's opinion, which it expressly stated applies to all Organization of American States (OAS) member states whether or not they are party to the American Convention on Human Rights, appears clearly to view natural law as a source of obligation. According to the Court: 'All persons have attributes inherent to their human dignity that may not be harmed; these attributes make them possessors of fundamental rights that may not be disregarded and which are, consequently, superior to the power of the State, whatever its political structure.' The Court nonetheless cited nineteen treaties and fourteen soft law instruments on the principle of non-discrimination, finding that taken together they evidence a universal obligation to respect and guarantee human rights without discrimination. On whether this principle amounts to *jus cogens*, the Court moved beyond the Vienna Convention, asserting that 'by its definition' and its development, *jus cogens* is not limited to treaty law.[22] The Court concluded that non-discrimination is *jus cogens*, being 'intrinsically related to the right to equal protection before the law, which, in turn, derives "directly from the

---

[22] 'In stating that *jus cogens* has been developed by international case law, the court wrongly cited to the ICJ judgments in the Application of the Convention of the Prevention and Punishment of the Crime of Genocide, Preliminary Objections (*Bosnia-Herzegovina v Yugoslavia*, ICJ Reports 1996, p. 595 and the Barcelona Traction, Light and Power Company, Second Phase, Judgment, ICJ Reports, p. 3, [neither of which discusses the subject].

oneness of the human family and is linked to the essential dignity of the individual"'. The Court added that the principle belongs to *jus cogens* because the whole legal structure of national and international public order rests on it and it is a fundamental principle that permeates all laws. The effect of this declaration, according to the Court, is that all states are bound by the norm *erga omnes*. The Court's opinion considerably shifts lawmaking from states to international tribunals which are asked to assess human dignity and international public order.

The Human Rights Committee addressed the implications of *jus cogens* in its General Comment No. 29 on States of Emergency, issued 31 August 2001. According to the Committee, the list of non-derogable rights in Article 4(2) of the Covenant on Civil and Political Rights is related to, but not identical with the content of peremptory human rights norms. While some non-derogable rights are included 'partly as recognition of the[ir] peremptory nature', other rights not included in Article 4(2) figure among peremptory norms. The Committee emphatically insisted that 'States parties may in no circumstances invoke Article 4 of the Covenant as justification for acting in violation of humanitarian law or peremptory norms of international law, for instance by taking hostages, by imposing collective punishments, through arbitrary deprivations of liberty or by deviating from fundamental principles of fair trial, including the presumption of innocence'.[23] While this may appear to be adding new conditions to Article 4, in fact paragraph 1 explicitly provides that any measures taken by states in derogation of Covenant rights must not be 'inconsistent with their other obligations under international law'. In terms of consequences of this extension, the Committee asserts that one test of the legitimacy of measures in derogation of Covenant rights can be found in the definition of certain violations as crimes against humanity. Thus, the fact that the Covenant would appear on its fact to permit such measures cannot be invoked as a defence to individual criminal responsibility.

7.2 Accountability

Apart from potentially rendering void international agreements, *jus cogens* has sometimes been invoked in an effort to hold accountable individuals

---

[23] General Comment No. 29, para. 11.

or states for the commission of unilateral acts allegedly in violation of per-emptory norms. Sir Peter von Hagenbach, Governor of the Austrian town of Breisach from 1469 to 1474, was tried and beheaded on May 9, 1474, for crimes against the 'laws of God and humanity [Man]'. His crimes included rape, murder, and destruction of property during peacetime. General Telford Taylor, US prosecutor at the Nuremberg Military Tribunal, cited the Hagenbach trial to support prosecution for the commission of 'crimes against humanity' as a recognized principle of international law:

> It needs no elaborate research to ascertain that international penal law has long recognized the international character of certain types of atrocities and offenses shocking to the moral sense of all civilized na-tions ... The Public Prosecutor, Henry Iselin of Basel, Switzerland, ac-cused Sir Peter of having committed deeds which outraged all notions of humanity and justice and constituted crimes under natural law; in the words of the prosecutor, the accused had 'trampled underfoot the laws of God and men'.[24]

In various domestic courts, lawyers have argued that the foreign sovereign immunity must make way for accountability, that is, it must be interpreted to include an implied exception to sovereign immunity for violations of *jus cogens* norms. The argument relies on the idea of implied waiver, positing that State agreement to elevate a norm to *jus cogens* status inherently results in an implied waiver of sovereign immunity. Every court thus far has re-jected the argument and upheld immunity, although some judicial panels have split on the issue.[25]

In the case of former Chilean leader, Augusto Pinochet Ugarte, the issue of *jus cogens* was pressed in response to a claim of immunity from criminal prosecution. Among the many opinions in the case, Lord Millett stated that '[i]nternational law cannot be supposed to have established a crime having

---

[24] See *US v Ernst von Weizsaecher*, Trials of War Criminals before the Nuremberg Military Tribunals under Control Council Law No. 10, IMT Ministries Case No. 11/Vol. 13, October 1946–October 1949, at 96–97. See also *US v von Leeb*, Trials of War Criminals before the Nuremberg Military Tribunals under Control Council Law No. 10, The High Command Case No. 12/Vol. 11, October 1946–May 1949, at 476. The number of judges who presided at the Hagenbach trial differs in several accounts from 26 to 28 judges, but there is agreement that the judges were drawn from different states, providing support to the widely held view that the trial was held before an international ad hoc tribunal.

[25] See, e.g. *Siderman v The Republic of Argentina*, 965 F.2d 699 (9th Cir. 1992), cert. denied, 113 S Ct 1812 (1993).

the character of a *jus cogens* and at the same time to have provided an immunity which is co-extensive with the obligation it seeks to impose'.[26] The judgment ultimately did not rely on *jus cogens* to determine the issue, however, because the situation was controlled by the relevant treaty.

Four recent cases from different national courts demonstrate the confusion over *jus cogens* and its relationship to issues of immunity. In all of the cases the courts held that the underlying violations constituted breaches of norms *jus cogens*—two cases involved war crimes and two concerned torture—but the courts split evenly on whether a finding of *jus cogens* violations results in overriding traditional immunity. In a case from Greece and one from Italy, the respective supreme courts held that German crimes committed during World War II were not protected by sovereign immunity.[27] In contrast, an Ontario, Canada Court of Appeal and an English appellate tribunal held that the *jus cogens* prohibition of torture does not override sovereign immunity.[28]

a. Issues of hierarchy: Resolving priorities between conflicting norms

Systems of law usually establish a hierarchy of norms based on the particular source from which the norms derive. In national legal systems, it is commonplace for the fundamental values of society to be given constitutional status and afforded precedence in the event of a conflict with norms enacted by legislation or adopted by administrative regulation; administrative

[26] *R v Bow Street Metropolitan Stipendiary Magistrate and others, ex parte* Pinochet Ugarte [1999] 2 All ER 97 (HL) at 179.

[27] See *Prefecture of Voiotia v Federal Republic of Germany*, Case No. 11/2000 (Areios Pagos, Supreme Court of Greece, 4 May 2000) and *Ferrini v Federal Republic of Germany*, Italian Corte di Cassazione (Sezioni Unite) Judgment no. 5044 of 6 November 2003, registered 11 March 2004 (2004) 87. The Italian case is discussed in P. De Sena and F. De Vittor, 2005, 'State immunity and human rights: The Italian Supreme Court decision on the *Ferrini* Case', *16 Eu. J. Int'l Law* 89. In the subsequent *Lozano* case, decided in July 2008, the Italian Corte di Cassazione gave preference to the functional immunity of a state agent over allegations that he had committed a war crime, on the ground that only grave breaches of humanitarian law constitute war crimes such as to override immunity. Such breaches require large-scale, odious, and inhuman intentional acts; lesser acts do not constitute an international crime. The court referred to the peremptory nature of international humanitarian law in respect to grave breaches. For a summary and critique of the judgment, see A. Cassese, 2008, 'The Italian court of cassation misapprehends the notion of war crimes', 6 *J. Int'l Criminal Justice* 1077.

[28] See *Bonzari v Iran*, Ontario Court of Appeal, OJ No. 2800 (2004), 1991-1 Feuille fédérale, pp. 440–442 and *Jones v Saudi Arabia*, EWCA Civ. 1394 (2004).

rules themselves must conform to legislative mandates, while written law usually takes precedence over unwritten law and legal norms prevail over non-legal (political or moral) rules. The mode of legal reasoning applied in practice is thus naturally hierarchical, establishing relationships and order among normative statements and levels of authority.[29] In practice, conflicts among norms and their interpretation are probably inevitable in the present, largely decentralized, international legal system where each state is entitled initially and equally to interpret for itself the scope of its obligations and how to implement such obligations.

Some scholars argue, based on the ICJ Statute and the idea of sovereign equality of states, that no hierarchy exists and logically there can be none: international rules are equivalent, sources are equivalent, and procedures are equivalent, all deriving from the will of states.[30] Others point to the concept of the community of states as a whole, expressed in Article 53 VCLT, as an emerging limit on unilateral relativism.[31] The ILC study group on fragmentation of international law concluded that hierarchy does exist in international law with norms of *jus cogens* superior to other rules on account of their contents as well as the universal acceptance of their superiority.[32]

States have agreed on the means (or 'sources') to identify binding international obligations for the purpose of resolving their disputes, but they have not determined a hierarchy of norms. As formulated initially in the Statute of the Permanent Court of International Justice (PCIJ) and iterated in the ICJ Statute, the Court should decide an international dispute primarily through the application of international conventions, international custom, and general principles of law. The Statute makes no reference to hierarchy, except by listing doctrine and judicial decisions as 'subsidiary' and evidentiary sources of law. Although the Statute is directed at the Court, it is the only general text in which states have acknowledged the authoritative procedures by which they agree to be legally bound to an international norm. No mention is made of *jus cogens* as a source of obligation, nor do non-binding instruments figure in the Statute.

The ILC Articles on State Responsibility (ASR) and accompanying Commentary acknowledge that the issue of hierarchy of norms has been

---

[29] M. Koskenniemi, 1997, 'Hierarchy in international law: A sketch', *8 Eur. J. Int'l Law* 566–582.

[30] P.-M. Dupuy, 1995, *Droit International Public* (3rd edn, Paris, Dalloz), pp. 14–16.

[31] Salcedo (n 7), 588.

[32] Fragmentation of international law, paras 31–32.

much debated, but find support for *jus cogens* in the notion of *erga omnes* obligations, the inclusion of the concept of peremptory norms in the Vienna Convention on the Law of Treaties, in international practice and in the jurisprudence of international and national courts and tribunals.[33] Article 41 ASR sets forth the particular consequences said to result from the commission of a serious breach of a peremptory norm. To a large extent Article 41 ASR seems to be based on United Nations practice, especially actions of the Security Council in response to breaches of the UN Charter in Southern Africa and by Iraq. The text refers to positive and negative obligations of all States. In respect to the first, '[w]hat is called for in the face of serious breaches is a joint and coordinated effort by all states to counteract the effect of these breaches'. The Commentary concedes that the proposal 'may reflect the progressive development of international law' as it aims to strengthen existing mechanisms of cooperation. The core requirement, to abstain from recognizing consequences of the illegal acts, finds support in state practice with precedents including rejection of the unilateral declaration of independence by Rhodesia, the annexation of Kuwait by Iraq, and the South African presence in Namibia. Article 41 ASR extends the duty to combat and not condone, aid, or recognize certain illegal acts beyond those acts that breach the UN Charter.

The jurisprudence of national and international courts on sovereign immunity and *jus cogens* lessen considerably the potential function of the latter norms to enhance accountability, but the courts were faced with unpalatable alternatives. They could have declared sovereign immunity to be a *jus cogens* norm equal in value to the prohibition of torture or war crimes, which would likely have generated considerable disquiet about elevating the rights of states to a level equal to that of non-derogable human rights and humanitarian norms. Alternatively, the courts could have refrained from pronouncing on the substantive norms as *jus cogens*, despite the centrality of the issue to the cases before them. The resulting judgments would probably have been even more questionable in reasoning than is the artificial and unconvincing distinction between substantive and procedural norms. As a third alternative, the courts could have stepped back to examine the issue of sovereign immunity in the larger context of sovereign equality of states, a fundamental norm of the international community, and considered the underlying public policies favouring sovereign immunity,

---

[33] Draft articles on responsibility of States for internationally wrongful acts, with commentaries, at pp. 84–85.

such as avoiding politically motivated lawsuits or prejudicial forums that could exacerbate hostility between states and threaten international peace and security. Acknowledging that fundamental values were engaged by both norms could have led to a balancing to resolve the conflict allowing for a narrow judgment restricted to the facts of each case.

7.3 Declaration of Fundamental Values

The main appearance of *jus cogens* in jurisprudence thus far has been predominately expressive, to declare that certain norms fall within the doctrine because of their content. Several scholars also support a declarative function for *jus cogens*, one that permits the expression of fundamental values. ILC member Mustafa Kamil Yaseen commented that 'the only possible criterion' for distinguishing peremptory norms from ordinary conventional or customary norms 'was the substance of the rule', including whether the norms were 'deeply rooted in the international conscience'.[34] Louis Henkin and Louis Sohn similarly suggested that *jus cogens* norms derive their peremptory character from their inherent rational and moral authority.[35] Bianchi more pointedly comments that the primary function of *jus cogens* has been symbolic or expressive of fundamental values: 'By fostering a political and normative project, clearly at odds with the paradigms of the past, *jus cogens* has produced a moral force of unprecedented character'.[36] The evidence to date supports this thesis.

In jurisprudence, *jus cogens* has been used to signal that the norm in question reflects particularly important values in the eyes of the judges. The ICJ endorsed *jus cogens* its 2006 Judgment on Preliminary Objections in *Armed Activities on the Territory of the Congo* (*Congo v Rwanda*).[37] The Court stated that the prohibition of genocide is 'assuredly' such a norm, but the Court emphasized that the *jus cogens* status of the prohibition of genocide did not have an impact on its jurisdiction, which remains governed by consent. A dissenting opinion questioned whether the *jus cogens*

---

[34] International Law Commission, Summary records of the 673rd to 685th plenary meetings, 6–22 May 1963, A/CN.4/SR.673–685, at 63.

[35] L. Henkin, 1981, *The International Bill of Rights: The Covenant on Civil and Political Rights* (New York, Columbia University Press), p. 15; L.B. Sohn, 1982, 'The new international law: Protection of the rights of individuals rather than states', *32 Am. University Law Rev.*, 1–61.

[36] A. Bianchi, 2008, 'Human rights and the magic of *jus cogens*', *19 Eur. J. Int'l Law* 491, 496.

[37] *Armed Activities on the Territory of the Congo.*

prohibition of genocide meant that a reservation to the Court's jurisdiction might be incompatible with the object and purpose of the Genocide Convention, but other judges declined to pronounce on the matter. In dicta in the *Jurisdictional Immunities* case, the Court added unnecessarily it would seem that it could not find a *jus cogens* norm requiring full compensation be paid to each individual victim of an armed conflict.

The declaratory function was perhaps made most clear by the ICTY, the first international tribunal to discuss *jus cogens* and declare the prohibition of torture as one such norm. The Court said it did so 'because of the importance of the values [the prohibition against torture] protects', which makes it a norm that enjoys a higher rank in the international hierarchy than treaty law and even 'ordinary' customary rules. Clearly, the *jus cogens* nature of the prohibition against torture articulates the notion that the prohibition has now become one of the most fundamental standards of the international community.[38] This *jus cogens* declaration had no bearing on the guilt or innocence of the person on trial, nor on the binding nature of the law violated, nor, apparently on the range of punishments. It was not asserted that any treaty or local custom was in conflict with the customary and treaty prohibition of torture. The reference served a rhetorical purpose only.

The declarative or expressive function of *jus cogens* need not mean the absence of practical consequences or effects. As Bianchi notes, 'symbols reflect the values imposed by the prevailing social forces. However, once they materialize and become the pivotal structures of society, they may in turn coerce the power of the very same social forces from which they emanate'.[39] For decision-makers, *jus cogens* may thus cause them to pay greater attention to implementing effectively the underlying values: 'What matters most is not that the rule takes formal precedence in case of conflict, but rather the modalities of implementation of the underlying value, which ought to be given precedence at the interpretive level'.[40] *Jus cogens* can thus provide a means to balance interests and interpret legal obligations in ways that affirm 'the emergence of values which enjoy an ever-increasing recognition in international society'.[41] Systematically interpreting rules and principles

---

[38] *Prosecutor v Furundzija*, Trial Chamber, Judgment, Case No. IT-95–17/1-T, 10 December 1998, para. 153.

[39] Bianchi (n 36) at 507.

[40] Ibid., at 504.

[41] *Arrest Warrant of 11 April 2000 (Democratic Republic of the Congo v Belgium)*, ICJ, Judgment of 14 February 2002, Joint separate opinion of Judges Higgins, Kooijmans, and Buergenthal, para. 73.

in this way, to reflect the international normative, may help to resolve complex cases of potentially conflicting norms.

7.4 Concluding Remarks

Notwithstanding countless scholarly articles and its inclusion in the VCLT, the origins, contents and legal effects of *jus cogens* remain ill-defined and contentious. Its precise nature, what norms qualify as *jus cogens* and the consequences of *jus cogens* in international law remain unclear.[42] In 1993, the Commission declined to proceed with a study of the topic. Commissioner Bowett expressed his doubt as to whether the Commission's consideration of *jus cogens* would 'serve any useful purpose at this stage' because practice on *jus cogens* 'did not yet exist' it would be 'premature for [the Commission] to enter into this kind of study'. In 2014, the ILC decided that enough development had occurred in practice to make it worthwhile to study the issue of *jus cogens*,[43] although most of the practice appears negative as far as explaining the origin or consequences of the concept.

One purpose of asserting that a norm is *jus cogens* seems to be to override the will of persistent objectors to a norm of customary international law. The problem of imposing norms on non-consenting states has long troubled scholars and seems to be a matter of increasing urgency. Yet, the problem of dissenting states is not as widespread as might be assumed. First, the obligations deemed basic to the international community—to refrain from the use of force against another state, to settle disputes peacefully, and to respect human rights, fundamental freedoms, and self-determination— are conventional obligations contained in the UN Charter, to which all member states have consented. The multilateral regimes for the oceans, outer space, and key components of the environment are also widely accepted. Thus, in most cases the problem is one of ensuring compliance by

---

[42] The International Law Commission has twice discussed the question of doing further work on this topic. In the 1993 Commission Andreas Jacovides presented a paper to a Working Group of the Planning Group on *jus cogens* as a possible ILC topic, noting that 'no authoritative standards have emerged to determine the exact legal content of *jus cogens*, or the process by which international legal norms may rise to peremptory status'. More recently, the ILC's report on fragmentation of international law stated as follows: 'disagreement about [*jus cogens*] theoretical underpinnings, scope of application and content remains as ripe as ever'. Fragmentation of international law, para. 363.

[43] International Law Commission, Report of the International Law Commission, *Jus cogens* (Mr D. Tladi), 66th sess., UN Doc. A/69/10 Annex, 2014.

states with obligations they have freely accepted and not one of imposing obligations on dissenting states.

The question of dissenters could arise in the future if the number of purported norms *jus cogens* grows in an effort to further the common interests of humanity. The literature is replete with claims that particular international norms form part of *jus cogens*. Proponents have argued for inclusion of all human rights, all humanitarian norms (human rights and the laws of war), the duty not to cause transboundary environmental harm, the duty to assassinate dictators, the right to life of animals, self-determination, and territorial integrity (despite legions of treaties transferring territory from one state to another).

The concerns raised are serious ones, for the most part, and the rationale that emerges from the literature is one of necessity and increasing recognition of fundamental values: it is asserted that the international community cannot afford a consensual regime to address many modern international problems. Thus, *jus cogens* is a necessary development in international law, required because the modern interdependence of states demands an international *ordre public*. The ILC Commentary on the articles on State responsibility favours this position, asserting that peremptory rules exist to 'prohibit what has come to be seen as intolerable because of the threat it presents to the survival of states and their peoples and the most basic human values'.[44] The urgent need to act that is suggested fundamentally challenges what most scholars and certainly states see as the consensual framework of the international system. State practice has yet to catch up with this plea of necessity and it has been international and national courts which have pushed the concept forward. In short, while the *jus cogens* concept has achieved widespread acceptance across the international community, its unsettled theoretical foundation has impeded its implementation and development. For *jus cogens* to achieve full legal standing, it will need to be framed in a way that illuminates its normative origins, achieves agreement on its functions, and explains its relationship to state consent.

Finally, there are similarities between the assertions of *jus cogens* and the consequences of writing about fictional detectives like Sherlock Holmes, in regard to the limited impact of both. It appears that neither police investigations nor state practices have been substantially altered by these creations. Yet, both have had an undeniable impact on their respective cultures.

---

[44] Draft articles on State responsibility, para. 3.

Detective fiction remains a staple of the literature, while film incarnations of Sherlock Holmes seemingly appear every generation. In law, hundreds of articles and dozens of books have been devoted to *jus cogens*, or argue for the elevation of particular norms to this higher status. In sum, it seems that *jus cogens*, like Sherlock Holmes, serves mainly as a cultural or literary concept that has assumed a certain limited reality. It expresses belief in a core set of fundamental values and in the existence of an international society accepting of those values. Substantial legal impacts may yet arrive, because literary creations can and do influence society. Like the tourists who flock to Baker Street convinced of the reality of Sherlock Holmes, adherents of *jus cogens* may continue to expect it to have an impact in the real world.

References

UN Documents

Report of the International Law Commission on its 66th Session (2014), GAOR Sixty-ninth Session, Supplement No. 10 UN Doc A/69/10.

Report of the International Law Commission on its 67th Session (2015), GAOR Seventieth Session, Supplement No. 10, UN Doc. A/70//10.

Report of the International Law Commission on its 68th Session, GAOR Seventy-first Session (2016), Supplement No. 10, UN Doc. A/71/10.

Report of the International Law Commission on its 69th Session (2017), GAOR Seventy-second Session, Supplement No. 10, UN Doc. A/72/10.

Report of the International Law Commission on its 70th Session (2018), UN GAOR Seventy-third Session, Supplement No. 10, UN Doc. A/73/10.

Report of the International Law Commission on its 71st Session (2019), UN GAOR Seventy-fourth Session, Supplement No. 10, UN Doc. A/74/10.

First Report of Mr. Dire Tladi, Special Rapporteur on *Jus cogens*, ILC Sixty-eighth Session, UN Doc. A/CN.4/693 (2016)

Second Report of Mr. Dire Tladi, Special Rapporteur of the ILC on Peremptory Norms of General International Law (*Jus cogens*), UN Doc. A/CN.4/706.

Third Report of Mr. Dire Tladi, Special Rapporteur of the ILC on Peremptory Norms of General International Law (*Jus Cogens*), UN Doc. A/CN.4/714 and Corr.1.

Fourth Report of Mr. Dire Tladi, Special Rapporteur of the ILC on Peremptory Norms of General International Law (*Jus Cogens*), UN Doc. A/CN.4/727.

UNGA Res. 70/236 of 23 December 2015; Res. 71/140 of 13 December 2016; Res. 72/116 of 7 December 2017.

Vienna Convention on the Law of Treaties, 1155 UNTS 331; 1986 Vienna Convention on the Law of Treaties between States and International Organizations or between International Organizations, UN Doc. A/CONF.129/15.

H. Lauterpacht, Special Rapporteur, Report on the law of treaties, UN Doc. A/CN.4/63, 24 March 1953.

Report of the proceedings of the Committee of the Whole, UN Doc. A/CONF.39/11, 21 May 1968, at 471–472 (comments of the chairman).

Report of the Study Group of the International Law Commission, 58th Sess., UN Doc. A/CN.4/L.682, 13 April 2006, at 181.

J.L. Brierly, Special Rapporteur, Report on the law of treaties, UN Doc. A/CN.4/23, 14 April 1950, at 246 ff.

International Law Commission, Report of the International Law Commission on the work of the second part of its 17th sess., 17th sess. of the ICL, UN Doc. A/6309/Rev.1, 3–28 January 1966, at 247 ff.

International Law Commission, draft articles on the responsibility of States for internationally wrongful acts, with commentaries, 53rd sess. of the ILC, UN Doc. A/56/10, 2001, at 84–85.

H. Lauterpacht, Special Rapporteur, Report on the Law of Treaties: Legality of the object of the treaty, 5th sess. of the ILC, UN Doc. A/CN.4/63, 24 March 1953, Art. 15, at 154 (emphasis added).

Sir H. Waldock, Special Rapporteur, Second report on the Law of Treaties: Treaties void for illegality. 15th sess. of the ILC, UN Doc. A/CN.4/156 and Add.1–3, 1963, Article 13(3), at 52.

International Law Commission, Guide to practice on reservations to treaties with commentaries, 63rd session of the ILC, UN Doc. A/66/10/Add.1, 2011.

Principle 8 of the International Law Commission, Guiding principles applicable to unilateral declarations of states capable of creating legal obligations, with commentaries thereto, 58th sess. of the ILC, UN Doc. A/61/10, 2006, Principle 8.

International Law Commission, Report of the International Law Commission, *Jus cogens* (Mr D. Tladi), 66th sess., UN Doc. A/69/10 Annex, 2014.

Books and Articles

Ago, R. (1971) Droit des traités à la lumière de la Convention de Vienne, *134 Collected Courses of The Hague Academy of Int'l Law* 324.

Akehurst, M. (1974–1975) The hierarchy of the sources of international law, *47 Br Yearb. Int'l Law* 273–285.

Alexidze, L. (1981) The legal nature of jus cogens in contemporary international law, *Collected Courses of the Hague Academy of Int'l Law*, vol. 172, pp. 219–270

Allain, J. (2001) The *jus cogens* nature of non-refoulement, *13 Int'l J. Refugee Law* 533–558.

Al-Shible, M. (2018) The role of the advisory opinion of the International Court of Justice in establishing the rules of international humanitarian law, *72 J. Law, Policy and Globalization* 107–110.

Amnon, A. (2012) *Tracing the Earliest Recorded Concepts of International Law: The Ancient Near East (2500–330 BC)* (Leiden, Nijhoff).

Bassiouni, M.C. (1996) International crimes: *jus cogens* and obligations erga omnes, *59 Law and Contemporary Problems* 63–74.

Bassiouni, M.C. (1999) *Crimes against Humanity in International Criminal Law* (2nd rev. edn, The Hague, Martinus Nijhoff), p. 348.

Besner, J. and Attaran, A. (2008) Civil Liability in Canada's Courts for Torture Committed Abroad: The Unsatisfactory Interpretation of the State Immunity Act of 1985, *16 Tort Law Rev.* 150–167.

Bianchi, A. (2008) Human rights and the magic of *jus cogens*, *19 Eur. J. Int'l Law* 491–508.

Birnie, P., Boyle, A., and Redgwell, C. (2009) *International Law and the Environment* (3rd edn, Oxford, Oxford University Press), pp. 109–110.

Brierly, J.L. (1936) Régles générales de droit de la paix, *58 Recueil des Cours* 5–242.

Brownlie, I. (1998) *Principles of Public International Law* (5th edn, Oxford, Oxford University Press).

Byers, M. (1997) Conceptualizing the relationship between *jus cogens* and erga omnes rules, *66 Nordic J. Int'l Law* 211–239.

Cançado Trindade, A.A. (2008) *Jus cogens*: The determination and the gradual expansion of its material content in contemporary international case-law, *35 Curso de Derecho Internacional (Organization of American States, Inter-American Juridical Committee)* 3–30.

Cançado Trindade, A.A. (2012) Enforced disappearances of persons as a violation of *jus cogens*: The contribution of the Inter-American Court of Human Rights, *81 Nordic J. Int'l Law* 507–536.

Cançado Trindade, A.A. (2013) *El Ejercicio de la funcion judicial internacional: Memorias de la Corte. Interamericano de Derecho Humanos* (3rd edn, Belo Horizonte, Brazil, Del Rey Publications).

Cardoso Squeff, T. de A.F.R. and Almeida Rosa, M. (2018) *Jus Cogens*: An European Concept? An Emancipatory Conceptual Review from the Inter-American System of Human Rights, *15 Brazilian J. Int'l Law* 124–137.

Carnegie Endowment for International Peace (1967) *The Concept of* Jus Cogens *in International Law* (Geneva, Carnegie Endowment International Peace).

Cassese, A. (2008) The Italian Court of Cassation Misapprehends the Notion of War Crimes, *6 J. Int'l Criminal Justice* 1077.

Cassese, A. (2012) For an enhanced role of *jus cogens*. In: A. Cassese (ed.) *Realizing Utopia: The Future of International Law* (Oxford, Oxford University Press), pp. 158–171.

Cavare, L. (1962) *Droit international public positif* (2nd edn, Paris, Pedone).

Charlesworth, H. and Chinkin, C. (1993) The gender of *jus cogens*, *15 Human Rights Quarterly* 63–76.

Chinkin, C. (2006) *Jus cogens*, Article 103 of the UN Charter and other hierarchical techniques of conflict solution, *17 Finnish Yearb. Int'l Law* 63–90.

Chitty, J. (1849) Preface. In: E. de Vattel, *The Law of Nations; or Principles of the Law of Nature Applied to the Conduct and Affairs of Nations and Sovereigns* (transl. and intro. by J. Chitty (7th Am. edn, Philadelphia, T. & J.W. Johnson Law Booksellers), pp. vii–xvii.

Christenson, G.A. (1987–1988) *Jus cogens*: Guarding interests fundamental to international society, *28 Virginia J. Int'l Law* 585–648.

Christófolo, J.E. (2016) *Solving Antinomies between Peremptory Norms in Public International Law* (Geneva, Schulthess), p. 216.

Ciaccio, P.D. (2008) A Torturer's Manifesto? Impunity through Immunity in *Jones v The Kingdom of Saudi Arabia*, *30 Sydney Law Rev.* 551–564.

Clapham, A. (2007) The *jus cogens* prohibition of torture and the importance sovereign state immunity. In: M.G. Kohen (ed.) *Promoting Justice, Human Rights and Conflict Resolution through International Law: Liber amicorum Lucius Caflisch* (The Hague, Martinus Nijhoff), pp. 151–170.

Costelloe, D. (2017) *Legal Consequences of Peremptory Norms in International Law* (Cambridge, Cambridge University Press), p. 16.

Costello, C. and Foster, M. (2015) Non-refoulement as custom and *jus cogens?* Putting the prohibition to the test, *46 Neth. Yearb. Int'l Law* 273–323.

Cottier, T. (2015) Improving compliance: jus cogens and international economic law, *46 Neth. Yearb. Int'l Law* 133.

Criddle, E.J. and Fox-Decent, E. (2009) A fiduciary theory of *jus cogens, 34 Yale J. Int'l Law* 331–387.

Czaplin'ski, W. (1997–1998) Concepts of *jus cogens* and obligations *erga omnes* in international law in the light of recent developments, *23 Polish Yearb. Int'l Law* 87–97.

Czaplin'ski, W. (2006) *Jus cogens* and the law of treaties. In: C. Tomuschat and J.M. Thouvenin (eds) *The Fundamental Rules of the International Legal Order* (Leiden, Martinus Nijhoff), pp. 83–98.

d'Amato, A. (1990) It's a bird, it's a plane, it's *jus cogens, 9 Connecticut J. Int'l Law* 1–6.

Danilenko, G. (1991) International *jus cogens*: Issues of law-making, *2 Eur. J. Int'l Law* 42–65.

de Hoogh, A. (1991) The relationship between *jus cogens*, obligations *erga omnes* and international crimes: Peremptory norms in perspective, *42 Österreichische Zeitschrift für öffentliches Recht und Völkerrecht* 183–214.

de Hoogh, A. (1996) Obligations *erga omnes* and international crimes. Kluwer Law International, The Hague.

de Page, H. (1962) *Traité élémentaire de droit civil belge* (Brussels, Bruylant).

De Sena, P. and De Vittor, F. (2005) State Immunity and Human Rights: The Italian Supreme Court Decision on the *Ferrini* case, *16 Eu. J. Int'l Law* 89.

de Vattel, E. (1758) *Le droit des gens ou principes de la loi naturelle* (London, Neuchâtel).

de Vattel, E. (1849) *The Law of Nations; Or Principles of the Law of Nature Applied to the Conduct and Affairs of Nations and Sovereigns* (transl. and intro. by J. Chitty, 7th Am. edn, T. & J.W. Philadelphia, Johnson Law Booksellers).

de Wet, E. (2004) The prohibition of torture as an international norm of *jus cogens* and its implications for national and customary law, *15 Eur. J. Int'l Law* 97–121.

de Wet, E. (2006) The emergence of international and regional value systems as a manifestation of the emerging international constitutional order, *19 Leiden J. Int'l Law* 611–632.

de Wet, E. (2013) *Jus cogens* and obligations *erga omnes*. In: D. Shelton (ed.) *The Oxford Handbook on International Human Rights Law* (Oxford, Oxford University Press), pp. 541–561.

de Wet, E. and Vidmar, J. (eds) (2012) *Hierarchy in International Law: The Place of Human Rights* (New York, Oxford University Press).

Delbez, L. (1964) *Les principes generaux du droit international public* (3rd edn, Paris, Pichon et Durand-Auzias).

den Heijer, M. and van der Wilt, H. (2015) *Jus cogens* and the humanization and fragmentation of international law, *46 Neth. Yearb. Int'l Law* 3–21.

Donohue, L. (2008) *The Cost of Counterterrorism: Power, Politics and Liberty* (Cambridge, Cambridge University Press).

Dörmann, K. (2002) *Elements of War Crimes under the Rome Statute of the International Criminal Court* (Cambridge, Cambridge University Press), p. 328.

Duffy, A. (2008) Expulsion to face torture? *Non-refoulement* in international law, *20 Int'l J. Refugee Law* 373–390.

Dugard, J. (2018) *Confronting Apartheid: A Personal History of South Africa, Namibia and Palestine* (Johannesburg, Jacana), pp. 86, 137.

Dupuy, P.-M. (1995) Droit international public, (3rd edn, Paris, Dalloz), pp. 14–16.

Dupuy, P.-M. (2005) Some reflections on contemporary international law and the appeal to universal values: A response to Martti Koskenniemi, *16 Eur. J. Int'l Law* 131–137.

Farmer, A. (2008) Non-refoulement and *jus cogens*: Limiting anti-terror measures that threaten refugee protection, *23 Georgetown Immigration Law J.* 1–38.

Focarelli, C. (2008) Promotional *jus cogens*: A critical appraisal of *jus cogens'* legal effects, *77 Nordic J. Int'l Law* 429–459.

Frizzo Bragato, F. (2014) Para além do discurso eurocêntrico dos dereito humanos: Contribuções da descolonialidade, *19 Revista novos estudos juridicos* 201–230.

Frowein, J.A. (2009) *Jus cogens* and obligations *erga omnes*. In: R. Wolfrum (ed.) *Max Planck Encyclopaedia of Public International Law*, vol. VI. (Oxford, Oxford University Press), pp. 443 ff.

Gastorn, K. (2017) Defining the imprecise contours of *jus cogens* in international law, *16 Chinese J. Int'l Law* 643–662.

Gentili, A. (1933) *De iure belli libri tres* (Oxford, Clarendon Press; London, H Milford).

Glennon, M.J. (2006) De l'absurdité du droit impératif (*jus cogens*), *110 Revue Générale de Droit International Public* 529–536.

Grotius, H. (1625) *On the law of war and peace (De jure belli ac pacis libri tres)* (1646 edn transl. by F.W. Kelsey, 1925, Oxford, Clarendon Press).

Guggenheim, P. (1953) *Traité de droit international public* (Genf, Georg).

Hall, W. (1924) *A Treatise on International Law* (8th edn, Oxford, Clarendon).

Hanna, M. (2018) The Substantive/Procedural Distinction: Law's Solution to the Problem of *Jus Cogens* in a World of Sovereign States, *19 German Law J.* 21–42.

Hannikainen, L. (1988) *Peremptory Norms (Jus Cogens) in International Law* (Helsinki, Finnish Lawyers' Publishing Co.).

Henkin, L. (1981) *The International Bill of Rights: The Covenant on Civil and Political Rights* (New York, Columbia University Press), p. 15.

Henkin, L. (1989) International law: Politics, values and functions, *216 Recueil des Cours* 9–416.

Hennebel, L. and Tigroudja, H. (2009) *Le particularisme interaméricain des droits de l'homme* (Paris, Pedone), pp. 271–311.

Hossain, K. (2005) The concept of *jus cogens* and the obligation under the UN Charter, *3 Santa Clara J. Int'l Law* 72–98.

Husik, I. (1925) The law of nature, Hugo Grotius, and the Bible, *2 Hebrew Union College Ann* 381–417.

Janis, M.W. (1988) The nature of *jus cogens*, *3 Connecticut J. Int'l Law* 359–363.

Kadelbach, S. (2015) Genesis, function and identification of *jus cogens* norms, *46 Neth. Yearb. Int'l Law* 147–172.

Kawasaki, A. (2006) A brief note on the legal effects of *jus cogens* in international law, *34 Hitotsubashi J. Law and Politics* 27–43.

Kearney, R.D. and Dalton, R.E. (1970) The treaty on treaties, *64 Am. J. Int'l Law* 495–556.

Kelsen, H. (1945) *General Theory of Law and State* (Cambridge, Harvard University Press).

Kleinlein, T. (2015) *Jus cogens* as the 'highest law'? Peremptory norms and legal hierarchies, *46 Neth. Yearb. Int'l Law* 110–197.

Knuchel, S. (2015) *Jus Cogens: Identification and Enforcement of Peremptory Norms* (Zurich, Schulthess), p. 41.

Koh, H.H. (1994) Reflections on refoulement and the Haitian Centers Council, *35 Harvard Int'l Law J.* 1–20.

Kolb, R. (2001) *Théorie du* jus cogens *international: essai de relecture du concept* (Paris, Presses Universitaires de France).

Kolb, R. (2005) *Jus cogens*, intangibilité, intransgressibilité, dérogation 'positive' et 'négative', *109 Revue Générale de Droit International Public* 305–329.

Kolb, R. (2009) Observations sur l'evolution du concept de *jus cogens*, *113 Revue Générale de Droit International Public* 837–850.

Kolb, R. (2015) *Peremptory International Law (*Jus Cogens*): A General Inventory* (Oxford, Hart).

Kornicker Uhlmann, E.M. (1998) State community interests, *jus cogens* and protection of the global environment: Developing criteria for peremptory norms, *11 Georgetown Int'l Environmental Law Rev.* 101–136.

Koskenniemi, M. (1997) Hierarchy in international law: A sketch, *8 Eur. J. Int'l Law* 566–582.

Koskenniemi, M. (2006) *From Apology to Utopia: The Structure of Legal Argument* (Cambridge, Cambridge University Press), pp. 307 ff.

Kotzé, L.J. (2015) Constitutional conversations in the Anthropocene: In search of environmental *jus cogens* norms, *46 Neth. Yearb. Int'l Law* 241–272.

Lauterpacht, H. (1937) Régles générales de droit de la paix, *62 Recueil des Cours* 95–422.

Linderfalk, U. (2015) Understanding the *jus cogens* debate: The pervasive influence of legal positivism and legal idealism, *46 Neth. Yearb. Int'l Law* 51–84.

Lukashuk, I.I. (1989) The principle *pacta sunt servanda* and the nature of obligation under international law, *83 Am. J. Int'l Law* 513–518.

McGregor, L. (2007) Torture and State Immunity: Deflecting Impunity, Distorting Sovereignty, *18 Eur. J. Int'l Law* 903–919.

McNair, A.D. (1961) *Law of Treaties* (Oxford, Clarendon Press).

Maia, C. (2009) Le *jus cogens* dans la jurisprudence de la Cour interamércaine des droits de l'homme. In: L. Hennebel and H. Tigroudja (eds) *Le particularisme interaméricain des droits de l'homme* (Paris, Pedone), p. 277.

Marochkin, S.Y. (2009) On the recent development of international law: Some Russian perspectives, *8 Chinese J. Int'l Law* 695–714.

Meron, T. (1986) On a hierarchy of international human rights, *80 Am. J. Int'l Law* 1–30.

Meron, T. (1993) Rape as a crime under international humanitarian law, *87 Am. J. Int'l Law* 424–428.

Mik, C. (2013) *Jus cogens* in contemporary international law, *33 Polish Yearb. Int'l Law* 27–93.

Morelli, G. (1951) *Nozioni di diritto internazionale* (Padova, CEDAM).

Nieto-Navia, R. (2003) International peremptory norms (*jus cogens*) and international humanitarian law. In: L.C. Vorah et al. (eds) *Man's Inhumanity to Man: Essays in Honour of A. Cassese* (The Hague, Kluwer Law International), pp. 595–640.

O'Connell, M.E. (2012) *Jus cogens*: International law's higher ethical norms. In: Childress III (ed.) *The Role of Ethics in International Law* (New York, Cambridge University Press), pp. 78–98.

Oppenheim, L. (1905) *International Law* (London, Longmans).

Orakhelashvili, A. (2006) *Peremptory Norms in International Law* (Oxford, Oxford University Press), pp. 56, 65.

Orakhelashvili, A. (2015) Audience and authority: The merit of the doctrine of *jus cogens*, *46 Neth. Yearb. Int'l Law* 115–146.

Parker, K. and Neylon, L.B. (1988–1989) *Jus cogens*: Compelling the law of human rights, *11 Hastings Int'l and Comparative Law Rev.* 411–464.

Pellet, A. (2006) Comments in response to Christine Chinkin and in defense of *jus cogens* as the best bastion against the excesses of fragmentation, *17 Finnish Yearb. Int'l Law* 83–89.

Pufendorf, S. (1710) Of law of nature and nations (Oxford, L. Lichfield for A. & J. Churchill), Oxford 51.

Reuter, P. (1961) Principes de droit international public, *103 Recueil des Cours, Hague Academy Int'l Law.*

Robinson, N.A. (2018) Environmental law: Is an obligation *erga omnes* emerging? Paper presented at a panel discussion at the UN, 4 June 2018.

Robledo, A.G. (1982) *El ius cogens internacional* (Mexico, Universidad Nacional Autónoma de México).

Robledo, A.G. (1982) Le ius cogens international: Sa genese, sa nature, ses fonctions, *172 Recueil des Cours* 9–217.

Rozakis, C. (1976) *The Concept of Jus Cogens in the Law of Treaties* (Amsterdam, North Holland Publishing Co.), p. 2.

Rubin, A.P. (2000–2001) Actio popularis, *jus cogens* and offenses erga omnes, *35 New Engl. Law Rev.* 265–272.

Sadat, L.N. (2018) A contextual and historical analysis of the International Law Commission's 2017 draft articles for a new global treaty on crimes against humanity, *16 J. Int'l Criminal Justice* 683–704.

Salcedo, J.A.C. (1997) Reflections on the hierarchy of norms in international law, *8 Eur. J. Int'l Law* 583–595.

Santalla Vargas, E. (2015) In quest of the practical value of jus cogens norms, *46 Neth. Yearb. Int'l Law* 211–239.

Sarkin, J. (2012) Why the prohibition of enforced disappearance has attained *jus cogens* status in international law, *81 Nordic J. Int'l Law* 537–583.

Scelle, G. (1932) *Précis de droit des gens* (Paris, Recueil Sirey).

Scelle, G. (1948) *Cours de droit international public* (Paris, Dormat-Montchrestien).

Scott, J.B. (2009) *The Spanish Origin of International Law. Francisco De Vitoria and His Law of Nations* (Oxford, Oxford University Press).

Shaw, M.N. (2008) *International Law* (5th edn, Cambridge, Cambridge University Press).

Shelton, D. (1986) Normative hierarchy of international law, *80 Am. J. Int'l Law* 291–323.

Shelton, D. (2014) International law and 'relative normativity'. In: M.D. Evans (ed.) *International Law* (4th edn, Oxford, Oxford University Press), ch. 5, pp. 142–172.

Shelton, D. (2015) Sherlock Holmes and the mystery of *jus cogens*, *46 Neth. Yearb. Int'l Law* 23–50.

Sivakumaran, S. (2012) *The Law of Non-International Armed Conflict* (Oxford, Oxford University Press), p. 249.

Sohn, L.B. (1982) The New International Law: Protection of the Rights of Individuals Rather Than States, *32 Am. University Law Rev.* 1–61.

Starrett, V. (1950) Introduction. In: Sir A. Conan Doyle, *The Adventures of Sherlock Holmes* (New York, The Heritage Press), pp. v–xviii.

Stephan, P.B. (2011) The political economy of *jus cogens*, Virginia Public Law and Legal Theory Research Paper No. 2011–14. http://ssrn.com/abstract=1780472. Accessed 25 Aug. 2020.

Suy, E. (1967) The concept of *jus cogens* in public international law. In: 'The concept of *jus cogens* in international law: papers and proceedings'. Report of a conference organized by the Carnegie Endowment for International Peace, Lagonissi, Greece, April 1966, Carnegie Endowment for International Peace, Geneva.

Suy, E. (2011) Article 53: treaties conflicting with a peremptory norm of general international law ('*jus cogens*'). In: O. Corten and P. Klein (eds) *The Vienna Convention on the Law of Treaties: A Commentary*, vol. II (Oxford, Oxford University Press), pp. 1224–1234.

Sztucki, J. (1974) Jus cogens *and the Vienna Convention on the Law of Treaties* (Vienna, Springer).

Talmon, S. (2012) *Jus Cogens* after *Germany v Italy*: Substantive and Procedural Rules Distinguished, *25 Leiden J. Int'l Law* 979–1002.

Tomuschat, C. (1993) Obligations arising for states without or against their will, *241 Recueil des Cours* 191–374.

Tomuschat, C. (2014) The case of *Germany v Italy* before the ICJ. In: Anne Peters et al. (eds) *Immunities in the Age of Global Constitutionalism* (The Hague, Martinus Nijhoff), p. 88.

Tomuschat, C. (2015) The Security Council and *jus cogens*. In: E. Cannizzaro (ed.) *The Present and Future of* Jus Cogens (Rome, Sapienza.

Tomuschat, C. and Thouvenin, J.-M. (eds) (2006) *The Fundamental Rules of the International Legal Order:* Jus Cogens *and Obligations* Erga Omnes (The Hague, Martinus Nijhoff).

Tunkin, G.I. (1965) *Theory of International Law* (Paris, Pedone).

Verdross, A. (1966) *Jus dispositivum* and *jus cogens* in international law, *60 Am. J. Int'l Law* 55–63.

Verhoeven, J. (2008) Sur les 'bons' et les 'mauvais' emplois du *jus cogens*, *3 Annuario Brasileiro de Direito Internacional* 133–160.

Vidmar, J. (2013) Rethinking *jus cogens* after *Germany v Italy*: Back to Article 53?, *60 Netherlands Int'l Law Rev.* 1–25.

Virally, M. (1966) Réflexions sur le *jus cogens*, *12 Annuaire Français de Droit International* 5–29.

von der Heydte, F.A. (1932) Die Erscheinungsformen des Zwischenstaatlichen Rechts: *Jus cogens* und *jus dispositivum* im Völkerrecht, *16 Zeitschrift für Völkerrecht* 461–487.

von Verdross, A. (1937) Forbidden treaties in international law: Comments on Professor Garner's report on 'The Law of Treaties', *31 Am. J. Int'l Law* 571–577.

Weatherall, T. (2015) Jus cogens: *International Law and Social Contract* (Cambridge, Cambridge University Press), p. 202.

Weil, P. (1983) Towards relative normativity in international law?, *77 Am. J. Int'l Law* 413–442.

Weisburd, M. (1995) The emptiness of the concept of *jus cogens*, as illustrated by the war in Bosnia-Herzegovina, *17 Michigan J. Int'l Law* 1–51.

Wolff, C. (1764) *Jus gentium methodo scientifica pertractorum [A scientific method for understanding the law of nations]* (transl. by J.H. Drake, S.J. Brown, ed., London, Clarendon Press).

Yang, X. (2006) *Jus cogens* and state immunity, *3 New Zealand Yearb. Int'l Law* 131–179.

Index

For the benefit of digital users, indexed terms that span two pages (e.g., 52–53) may, on occasion, appear on only one of those pages.